The Poets Library Vol X

Arthur H Stockwell

The Poets' Library

Arranged and Compiled
by
Arthur H. Stockwell

VOLUME X

LONDON
ARTHUR H. STOCKWELL, LTD.
29 LUDGATE HILL, E.C. 4

Publishers' Note

The arrangement of the Poems is in no way indicative of merit. Each Poem is accepted on the simple conditions of the Competition. As far as possible, the Poems appear alphabetically according to the names of the Authors.

Volume XI is in course of preparation, and writers are invited to submit their efforts. Full particulars and Entry Form free.

MADE AND PRINTED IN GREAT BRITAIN BY
M. F. ROBINSON & CO. LTD., AT THE LIBRARY PRESS, LOWESTOFT

CONTENTS

v

CONTENTS

The Divine Touch

The beauteous splendour all around me,
　The canopy of Autumn glory,
Made me stand in wonder, with full heart,
Feeling strangely happy, unwilling to depart
　From that scene of beauty.

Exultation ran all through me,
I walked with lightsome tread, drinking in the glory,
　Breathing fast, then with bated breath,
As enchanting tints my intense admiration did request.
　Such magical colour I'd never beheld,
　I was hoping the lane was still long to the end.

　　The kingly grandeur of the sea,
　　The azure beauty of the sky,
　　And even sunset's fiery glow,
　　Had not called forth my admiration,
　　Or filled me with such inspiration,
　　As that lane of Autumn glory.

　　I linger'd here and linger'd there,
　　Without worry, without care ;
　　Then thanksgiving overwhelmed my soul,
　　Poured out, soared up to Him alone,
　　Whose touch divine, artistic pow'r,
　　Had made that lane of glorious colour.

Tho' years roll, the time pass by,
  Memory will cling, sweet thoughts abide;
The serenity of an Autumn day
  Will from my mind ne'er fade away.
'Twill come to calm a troubled thought;
'Twill come with gold and scarlet fraught,
  At eventide to cheer the way;
'Twill come as the sun and shed its rays
To brighten a mind that is dim with age.

I. ADAMSON.

Apart

When you are gone,
Just like a violin laid down,
Minus its notes and thrills of sound,
    My heart is bound,
When you are gone.

When you come back,
Vibrating things
With notes that sing,
    My heart unflings,
When you come back.

A. L. A.

Paradise

O Love, You know too well the heart is weak !
So why permit me all my love to speak ?
You might have shared this uninvited gift
In such a way as not to let me drift
O'er depthless oceans, where I cannot give
A world and more of that for which we live.
The mystic Star and beaut'ous cloud-tipped Mountain,
Mute virgin Flow'r and Tree, each is a fountain
Of perfect Love, could I but emulate !
Pure thing I cannot even simulate !
Yet still I live, and strive, though it be vain,
To know this Love no man can ever gain.
But Life, You know too well that Death is sweet !
Then why not grant me now this one retreat ?
You might have spared me futile pain, instead
To bind me with this sterile cutting thread,
To feel the hurt of joy composed from grief,
And know that this is Your imposed relief.
And Death, what keeps You ling'ring in the gloom ?
You are the way . . . far from a morbid doom,
Immune from strife that blights this earthly tie. . . .
To some New Life where we shan't want to die.

A. Thompson-Allen.

Better Things

Ezek. 36. 11.   1 Cor. 2. 9.

When on the threshold of our life,
  Though all be bright and free from strife,
God's promise comes to you and me,
  " The best of all is yet to be."

As on life's journey we may press,
  Meeting with trials, cares, distress,
God's promise comes, so true and free,
  " The best of all is yet to be."

If now our life is free from care,
  Having great joys with friends to share,
God's promise still to us shall be,
  " The best of all thou yet shalt see."

Should disappointments come apace,
  The friends we've loved, perchance prove base,
There's comfort here for you and me,
  " The best of all is yet to be."

If suffering now shall be our lot,
  Remember, God has not forgot;
His grace extends to you and me,
  With promise of the best to be!

Then, as we near life's journey's end,
  Nor can on earthly joys depend
In His good time, to you and me
  God gives the best that is to be.

Agnes A. Addison.

Meditation

When, quiet, in my room I sit,
Window open to the night,
Night's cool breezes gently blowing,
Moon and stars all shining bright,

God can come within the stillness
Of my mind, subdued and still;
He can whisper words of comfort
To a full surrendered will.

Christ, I feel Thy presence near me,
Thou art with me all the time;
So my thoughts sustain and cheer me,
And my life seems all sublime.

When He said, " I'm always with you,"
Did He mean to include me?
Or was His promise just for those
Who followed Him through Galilee?

Praise His name! I know His Spirit
Can abide and stay with me,
For I'm sure it is His presence
Gives such joy and ecstasy.

Who but Christ can give such gladness,
Satisfaction, calm and peace?
Can the world, the flesh, the devil,
Make the storms of life to cease?

Jesus, Jesus, Blessed Jesus,
Come afresh and fill my soul;
Here I yield my life for service—
Take and sanctify the whole!

LESLIE ALMOND.

The Hope of a To-Morrow

Where would the joy of living be,
Should there be no To-morrow?
If in our hearts we could not see
A gleam of hope to borrow?
Though troubles may beset to-day;
Bow us with grief and sorrow,
The minutes, hours, soon pass away,
And bring to us To-morrow.

The darkest night may bring bright dreams;
The morn comes with persistence;
To-morrow's sun more brightly beams
From out of night's dark distance.
Though black the clouds, and dim the ray
Of hope that fails to find us,
Another day may chase away
The dark clouds right behind us.

To-day we're sad, we do not sing,
Sad thoughts we cannot banish;
To weary hearts the night will bring
Sweet sleep, and fears will banish.
Where grief has laid its mantle o'er
We're all alone in sorrow;
Our prayers to Heaven will upward soar
For better things To-morrow.

Some yesterdays perchance recall
A kiss of sweet-heart tender;
On some to-day's great joy may fall,
To us bright gladness render.

So, though to-day be drab and grey,
Let us, with faith ascending,
Believe and hope *To-morrow* may
Bring us a happy ending.

JAMES A. ALLEN.

Money Lore

My song bemoans, as you will learn,
  The power and pride of man,
The only reigning Sovereign
  Which weakens mortal clan.

It is about a dollar, or
  Some shillings, pounds, and pence ;
Whatever name you choose to call,
  Stands high on every fence.

The salts came first, with shiny shells,
  Their wives and girls adored ;
Then followed other country Belles,
  With vanity aboard.

And then, as time went tumbling by,
  And the world went rolling on,
The shells were used as barter for
  The fruit and golden corn.

Then, by degrees, too tedious far,
  In little verse to state,
The gold was coined from the bar,
  The shells to re-instate.

And now it is the only god
  That men delight to serve ;
The madness greed of money sod
  Are the temples of this earth.

A dollar, like the gentle rain,
  If used in serving others,
Brings sure return, with host of gain
  To bless us and our brothers.

One that I met in last decade,
  In tattered garments clad,
Is now a ruling potentate
  Thro' helping many a lad.

E. P. ALLEN.

Unadopted

Little houses, red and brown,
  Each side ;
Little breezes, up and down,
  There hide :
Such a very quiet street,
Never anyone to meet.

Little gardens, trim and bare,
  Each side ;
Little rays of light and shade
  There hide :
Such a very quiet street,
Isn't even policeman's beat.

A. L. A.

Solitude

E'en though I found the path to wealth,
  Unstinted praise for laurels won,
The heritage of perfect health,
  The slanting rays of morning sun,

Yet still I'd lack my heart's desire,
  In solitude to be alone,
If I found not, there to retire,
  A sacred place—a shrine unknown.

Well might I lose my strange unrest,
  If on the morrow I could build,
Within the wilderness, a nest,
  With tranquil peace my bosom filled.

My spirit then would leave this clay,
  Ascending where no ills betide,
No traitor's gate where lips betray,
  No seat of scorners to deride.

Transported from all earthly woe,
  My raptured soul, to realms upborne,
Should soar—a quiet space—and lo !
  Divine release, I sadly mourn.

No deadly sound my peace invades,
  My restful stillness I explore ;
The note of discord quickly fades,
  In silent wonder, I adore !

In sight of Heaven's Gate—no less—
  I pause : strange music, low and sweet,
Comes softly, like some light caress,
  To make my hour of bliss complete.

Hushed in the quietude of this hour,
  Enchanting strains of music cease ;
I catch again that mystic power—
  The darkness deepens—all is peace !

H. STUART ALLEN.

Freedom

Oh, not for me the town and city,
    Oh, not for me the constant surging throng ;
For captive birds I feel deep pity,
    Find nothing stirring in their plaintive song.

But give to me the wide, far-stretching veld,
    The misty blue of a far-distant hill,
For *there* that thing that is called freedom's felt,
    There, the wild birds, the air, with music fill.

To roam at will o'er slope and deep ravine,
    See here and there high lights of colour grand—
Orange and crimson, yellow and each green—
    The careless dabs of Nature's artist hand.

Freedom ! Ah, 'tis, indeed, a priceless thing,
    To be for ever prized with jealous care !
How can a bird for happiness still sing,
    When wrenched away is all that makes life fair ?

No, not for me the town and city
    No, not for me the constant surging throng :
For captive birds I feel deep pity,
    Find nothing stirring in their plaintive song.

                                        M. ARVY.

Cinema

Darkness, blue smoke-ringed, lies around us all.
Our temples throb with heat,
And eyes are strained.
Below, through myriad curls of drifting smoke
And changing atmospheres,
We see the stage,
Which now receives into its lofty space
The figure of a boy, fresh with the eagerness of youth.
Then the enchanted wonder of his voice
Pours like a crystal stream
Into the denseness of that vibrant heat,
Dispersing cloud and pain,
And, with the utter beauty of its youth,
Creating an unearthly loveliness,
Which gives us coolness where we suffered heat.
The atmosphere is changed and seems to move
With the refreshment of a zephyr breeze,
While still the liquid floating song outpours
In silver cadences which bring us peace.

No greater joy could thirst-mad wand'rer know,
When in the desert sands he finds a stream
To slake his thirst with grateful eagerness,
Than gave the loveliness of this pure song to me,
When poured, like moon-drenched dew,
Into that cloying agony of heat.

STEPHEN BAGNALL.

God is Divine

God is divine! He is the Mighty One
Who helps us in the time of deep distress.
He, the Epitome of all things good,
Is ever near to heal our hearts, and bless,
And lead us safely Home when day is done.

God is divine! Though worlds should fall in twain,
He is above all worlds. His love so rare,
Is never shaken by our petty thoughts.
We are His errant ones. Though we despair,
He knows we must return to Him again.

God is divine! In this I rest content.
His peace with me for ever more will be.
I will not doubt! I am His trusting child.
Whatever He thinks best, He'll give to me:
I know that all His gifts are Heaven-sent.

God is divine! His wisdom cannot fail,
Nor is He in the tempest's killing blast.
Men's thoughts have turned to hate, and furious things:
But He will guide us to His side, at last,
And light our footsteps by His Holy Grail.

VIOLET BARKER.

For Holy Communion—Hymn

Truly, O Christ, we drink Thy blood,
   And eat Thy flesh, while Thou'rt unseen;
And in this sacramental food
   Find life and strength and bliss serene.

Thy Essence, which no eye can see,
   Nor hand can touch, nor mind explore,
Is here in this great mystery;
   And meekly kneeling, we adore.

Reveal Thy Holy Presence now,
   And fill our souls with silent awe;
And while we 'neath Thine Altar bow,
   Incline our hearts to keep Thy Law.

The knowledge of our secret sin,
   Which puts Thee oft to open shame,
And breaks Thy heart, melts us within;
   But cleansing seek we in Thy Name.

O Saving Host, unspotted Priest,
   Who for our sins doth make redress,
Dwell in our hearts who share this feast,
   That we may share Thy holiness!

Grant Thy unworthy guests to know,
   From sins confest we've been set free;
And bounteously Thy life bestow,
   And keep our lives in purity.

Then cleans'd, refresh'd, we'll grateful rise,
　　Fill'd with the strength Thy grace imparts,
And onward press to win Life's Prize,
　　E'en Thee, Whose love has won our hearts.

And when, in triumph, from the skies
　　Thou com'st to claim Thy Ransomed Bride
For the Great Feast in Paradise,
　　In Her Thou wilt be glorified. Amen.

REV. ALBAN E. BELBODA

You Came to Me

You came to me, and all the world was changed!
More silvery moon ne'er shone upon the night;
The flowers shone mystic—white beneath its beams,
And all the hours were sped in soft delight.

You came to me, and all the world was hushed!
No sweeter love e'er touched my being's core;
The hours held magic charm beneath its spell,
This new-old love of ours ne'er found before.

You came to me, and all the world awoke!
More joyful strains ne'er pealed from lover's lute:
The flowers have blossomed forth beneath the sun—
To you, my dear, I give love's sweet salute.

VIOLET BARKER.

The Short-lived Spring

You were so fair when Spring walked by your side,
Gay youth and innocence personified ;
Inscrutable, your soul danced through the skies,
And whispering secret trembled in your eyes.

I loved. Sweet-breasted birds sang in my ear,
Melodious, joyful, exquisitely clear :
When you but looked at me, so nobly meek,
Like a caress you lay upon my cheek.

And when you spoke to me, so softly shy,
My heart was touched as by a fairy's sigh ;
But when you smiled at me—impassioned thrill !—
I was immortal then, and Time stood still

Spring's hand no longer touches you, dear child.
Inspired, foolish dreams, and violets wild,
And blossoms rare, betray the faith divine
Of glorious hopes and treasures to be mine.

But yesterday was bliss; to-morrow sighs :
Is only Spring for ever paradise ?
The hunger in my flesh cried out, " Oh, stay ! "
But Summer came—and Life passed as a day.

W. R. BETT.

Carol For Christmas Morning

Venite! Venite!
  And over the hill,
Come poor men and mighty,
  With mirth and good will!
  The frost is chill,
    And the fields are grey—
Gloria, gloria,
     Hodie!

Ho! kings, with your learning,
  Come hither and learn
How the bush that was burning
  Continued to burn:
  You shall discern
    Such a fire in the hay!
Gloria, gloria,
     Hodie!

Ho! John with the holly!
  Ho! Dick with the cow!
Here's wisdom and folly
  On pilgrimage now!
  Peter and plough,
    They're all on the way—
Gloria, gloria,
     Hodie!

Ho! poor men, and wise men,
  And men all forlorn!
Arise, O arise, men,
  Without any scorn!

For Truth is born,
And lieth in hay.
Gloria, gloria,
Hodie !

M. J. BIDDELL.

Love

What is Love ?
It is the soft sunshine filtering through the trees,
The perfume of the flowers wafted by the breeze.

It is the song of birds greeting, at morn, the light ;
The shining of the moonbeams in the silent night.

It is the magic that transfigures everything ;
Its mantle round true lovers it delights to fling.

It is the Soul enshrined behind a loved One's smile
And as it is, above all else, the thing worth while,
Cherish Love.

G. M. BOBBETT.

Truth

What is Truth and where to find her?
   That vexed question of the Mind
Comes sometime to all Life's Pilgrims,
   And the answer's hard to find.

Some will seek her in devotion
   To a cause that others say
Must be wrong, for, to their notion,
   Truth lies just the other way.

Strange that Truth should be reluctant
   To reveal herself to men;
It must be we do not see her
   When she comes within our ken.

Sometimes she is dressed in beauty,
   Often shrouded is in woe;
Ever stands alone, undaunted,
   Fearing neither friend nor foe.

Those who love come near her Presence,
   Those who serve come nearer still,
For she dwells within the portals
   Of the heart that seeks GOD's Will.
                G. M. BOBBETT.

Mylor

Leaden sky and dull-green sea,
Fresh young leaves on every tree,
Cattle browsing on the lea,
  On the way to Mylor.

Ancient church among the trees,
Rest, and peace and sweet heartsease
Breathe from thee, and sorrow flees
  When we come to Mylor.

Peaceful spirit, hov'ring where
Tree-tops whisper, green and fair,
Fain I'd rest my body there,
  By the church at Mylor.

Freed from care and trouble's stress,
Freed from sorrow's bitterness,
Leave me to the soft caress
  Of the breeze at Mylor.

Weary of the chastening rod,
I would leave my soul to God,
Lay me down below the sod,
  'Neath the Yew at Mylor.

MARGARET BOSSANCE BOREHAM.

Little Brown Sails

Little brown sails, where are you sailing,
  Far out on the wide, wide sea?
Little brown sails, the wind is wailing,
  You'd better come back to me;
    For a wailing wind means a storm, they say,
    So little brown sails, come home, and stay.

Little brown sails, the storm-cloud's broken,
  The sea's lashed up into foam!
Little brown sails, the wind-god's spoken—
  Never shall you see home!
    With fiendish glee, he roars to the sky—
    O little brown sails, good-bye! good-bye!
                MARGARET BOSSANCE BOREHAM.

My Reward

No empty praise on me bestowing,
Nor fame, nor riches, shall satisfy my soul;
The greatest prize for me, is knowing
That "Do your best" has been my goal.
                WILLIAM E. BOSTON.

That Letter

Have you sent that letter home?
  Not yet? Sit down and write without delay:
It matters not where'er you roam,
  Your thoughts should reach dear friends some day.

You don't know what to write?
  Just pause and think awhile:
No loss? no gain? no victory in sight?
  No words for those who miss your smile?

Say, that of them you constant think;
  Of homely things that cheer your way—
From joys and sorrows—do not shrink;
  Sit down and write without delay.

And those belovèd ones who long
  To read those simple lines, though few?
The joy to them, as love's sweet song,
  Returns a thousandfold to you.

WILLIAM E. BOSTON.

A Prayer

Give me eyes to see rich light
  That shines from so-named common things,
Give me ears to hear aright
  Sweet sounds that simple nature sings.

Give me a mind to think thoughts, wise,
  Clean, selfless, sordid-free,
That so within me may arise
  Desire to live life worthily.

Give me the hands to do small deeds
  Of kindness to my fellows sad ;
To help supply mankind its needs,
  To work that all around be glad.

WILLIAM E. BOSTON.

Within the Heart

A lonely hour is like a drink to me,
It always gives me something in exchange,
Something to contemplate and call my own,
For something I have lost, some vague delight
Born in the loneliness that follows pain,
To which I can look up to in the dark,
And worship in the light by following.
For much as I am strong and born to bear,
Partly thro' intuition and desire,
I am but human, and I need a guide,
Someone or something to infuse in me
A sense of greatness, to be always there,
Astride the branching sunbeams of the morn,
And lingering in the dying light at eve.
Nor I alone. How many sit and dream,
And, in the middle of the working world,
Find room for sad reflection, ample thought,
And change the dry aspect of everything
Into a rivulet of memory !
How many in the slow beat of the heart,
Define the measured harmony in men,
And wrap themselves against the outer cold,
In that same beating, that same harmony !

                                  LEONARD BRAZIER.

April

Glowing and golden
Spirit of Spring,
Buds scarce unfolden,
Blossoms you bring;
Glowing with splendour,
Youthtide your sign,
Golden and tender,
April divine.

Oh, you are coming with sunshine and mirth,
Blessing the world with the glory of birth,
Hiding the bareness of Winter's stark dearth,
Clothing in beauty your own mother earth.

How can we greet you,
Spirit of love?
Where may we meet you?
Blue skies above,
Green grass and flowers
Springing around,
Sunshine and showers,
There you are found.

W. BRISLEE.

I Loved a Woman Once, and She was Fair

I loved a woman once, and she was fair—
  The fairest, sweetest of all womankind
  A gracious form was hers, a gracious mind,
A soul God-filled with precious jewels rare.
" Dear Lord," I prayed, " keep her with tender care,
  Be Thou her shield from every angry wind ;
  In her pure heart may sin no lodgment find."
Greatly God loved her—and He heard my prayer.

Beside her grave, upon a forest hill,
  God's watchers stand, and guard its secret well :
    King never slept beneath a grander dome.
I'm old, but not my heart. I love her still ;
  And she loves me, and, where earth's ransomed dwell,
    Waits for the coming of her lover home.

She often sits with me at eventide.
  When night's dark shadows fall, and no one's nigh,
  And my thoughts turn to her with weary sigh
As turn they must, she glides unto my side,
And, like the old, old time, her soft hands hide
  In mine ; and thus, while hours pass swiftly by,
  We sit and dream, my love long-gone and I,
Two souls by one deep common thought allied.

Heaven then seems near when thus she comes to me ;
  And when she's gone, I feel her presence still,
    A breathing of her soul into my own—
A subtle power, strong as eternity,
  Making the sun shine brighter, and each hill
    A beaten pathway leading to the Throne.
J. T. BURGESS.

Tokens of Love

Thy voice !
To me it is the sweetest tone
A woman loved has ever known,
It makes my heart, when sad and lone,
  Rejoice.

Thy smile !
It seems to chase the clouds away,
And makes my heart feel strangely gay:
With thee I feel I want to stay
  Awhile.

Thy touch !
It is, to me, a gentle hand,
Leading me safe to lovers land ;
It seems to say, " I understand
  So much."

Thy kiss !
It teaches me I am adored
By one I fain would call my lord ;
It doth the purest joy afford,
  And bliss.

My love,
These tokens of thy love for me
Have made me thine eternally:
We'll share the life that is to be
  Above.

Above,
We'll understand why all we planned
Became a castle built of sand;
And in that pure and happy land,
Still love.

DOROTHY M. BURT.

Aftermath

Now comes the twilight to my heart,
And all around the shadows fall;
That Sun of which I was a part
Has set beyond the reach of all.

No more shall I, with happy tread,
Bask in his light along the way,
Nor laugh at foolish words he said,
Making them mine another day.

I hold the silence in my hand,
And shiver as the night wind blows.
Dimly then, I understand . . .
The darkness falls when daylight goes.

MURIEL BURTON.

Illusion

I wonder if the Angels' wings
Reflect the blue of Heaven's tinge?

Then I recall—there is no place
Called Heaven. All is rolling space.
The sky can never break in two!
How can an Angel's face peek thro'
Something that isn't there? And yet . . .
Are Angels ever desolate?

How blue the sky that is not there!
And wisdom smiles, yet still I stare. . . .

MURIEL BURTON.

Surrender

Father, Thou hast planned my life
In love immeasurable;
Thou, with wisdom infinite,
Dost work out each detail;
And Thy power is limitless
Thy purpose to fulfil.
My only part is to obey;
Lord, help me not to fail.

VIOLET BURTON.

The Corduroy Road [1]

It leads from the hill in the pasture-field,
Through the woods, to the meadow-lands,
Where the long lush wildgrass bends and sways
  Like a sea rolling high on the sands.

The balsams rear dark spires skyward;
  There's vivid velvet moss
Where the turned leaves of the poplar dance,
  Near the wintergreen's smooth glass.

The incense of pine and cedar-tree,
  The sweet scent of new-mown hay;
Mingle with pungent lichen breath
  In nature's pot-pourri.

A hollow sound from the swooping wings
  Of a night-hawk, as evening falls
The mad loon laughs on the distant lake,
  And clearly the whippoorwill calls.

---

[1] The pioneer farmers of Ontario built waggon-roads over marshy places on their farms, by placing logs or tree-trunks side by side. Such roads, owing to their appearance, are called " corduroy " roads.

The Cliffs at Fermain Bay, Guernsey

I stood on the cliffs at Fermain Bay,
And looked across to the other side,
While down in the valley, thick with fern,
The streamlet murmured gently by.
'Twas a wondrous day early in May:
The Bluebells were in fullest bloom,
Primroses peeped from beds of green,
The Violets shed their rich perfume.

The scent of flowers, the voice of wind,
The switch of sea and trees combined,
The song of birds, the buzz of bees,
Called to one's mind some grand refrain
Of music, with peace for its theme.
The winding path trailed in and out,
Thro' heather and thro' fern so green ;
The grass did dance or so it seemed.

The sky a wondrous sheet of blue,
The sea, its glass, nearly the same ;
While bungalows on the cliff-tops,
A background formed of red and grey.
An old-world picture 'twas, in short,
Set, in relief, against the sky ;
One seemed to catch the sound of wings
Of Angels as they floated by.

As to this music I did list,
I seemed to Heaven itself drawn near ;
I seemed the very song to hear,
Of all the Ransomed round the throne

They seemed to be playing their harps of gold,
And as they sang they seemed to say,
" 'Twas the Lord came down and kissed the ground
On the cliffs that morn at Fermain Bay."

B. CAIPHAS.

Renunciation

I will not let my age hamper thy youth,
Leave me, ere my eyes are dim, my cheeks wan,
My weakness needing thy strength to lean upon.
Remember me as when each rising sun
Called me to joyous life ; to work begun
With a glad song of thankfulness for you,
And for all that is beautiful and true.
After life's prime, Time speeds its flight ;
Morn's glory scarcely faded, ere 'tis night.
Beloved, I pray thee do not with me stay
 Until the closing of life's little day.

BLANCHE CARDEN.

Twilight

The day was slowly dying, and the evening star
Was shining ever brighter in the darkening skies ;
And my gaze would keep returning to that little gate afar,
Where I knew my love would soon appear before my
 longing eyes.
Oh ! lightly, lightly, she tripp'd across the dewy grass,
And sweetly, sweetly, she sang upon her way ;
Then I hurried up the hill to meet the pretty little lass,
And I kiss'd her in the twilight at the close of day.

Again the day is dying, and the evening star
Is shining like a jewel in the heavens above ;
But although my eyes still linger on that little gate afar
I know they ne'er again will see the lady of my love,
For softly, softly, she whispered me a last farewell,
And sadly, sadly, she closed her tear-dimm'd eyes ;
And yonder in the churchyard, where you hear the
 vesper-bell.
Beneath the yew-tree's shadow, there my love now
 lies.

       — CHATWIN.

Life's Stars

Stars that peep incessantly
Midst the perfect skies so clear,
Soothing slumbers patiently,
Waiting till the morn draws near.

Stars that lie in little cots,
Surrounded by their Heaven,
These we know as tiny tots,
With all their faults forgiven.

Stars that past the furrows trip,
Youthful hearts that beat so gay,
These, we know, our sorrows ease,
When we can no longer play.

Movie Stars, both young and old,
Countless lives illumine they;
Well-known stories they unfold—
Peaceful end to working day.

Falling Stars when they alight,
And misfortune is their fare,
Are like Shooting Stars at night,
That step out beyond the glare.

Stars that wink at us, serene,
Still a secret meaning hide;
Those who would that secret glean,
Find their efforts still denied.

Stars that mingle with the sick,
Sleep refuse, disdain to nod,
Better gems one could not pick—
Faithful duty done to God;

All Life's Stars, together, will
Up to Heaven light the way,
Guiding errant footsteps still
Nearer to the Perfect Day.

W. A. CRUZE

Alone

How can I live without you, my Love ?
  This life is too hard alone ;
    And the sad waves say
    To my heart all day.
  With their dreary, ceaseless moan,
" Alone, alone, alone for ever,
  Parted are ye for aye ;
    No more shall ye meet,
    And your loved one greet,
So go on your weary way."

Ah, no, come back, for I love you so !
  My heart is all crushed and torn ;
    Come back, O my Love,
    From the Heav'ns above
To your lover, sad and worn.
But ever I hear the endless lay,
  That swells and throbs in my brain.
    For the waves and sea,
    With mischievous glee,
  Still murmur the same refrain,
" Alone, alone," etc.

Then take me too, to my Love so true !
  I break from earth's trammels free,
    That I may find rest
    On your surging breast—
  Ah, take me to her, O Sea !
It will not be long, Love, now, not long,

Ere I see your face again,
　And we meet once more,
　　On the far-off shore,
Peace banishing all our pain.

But the winds and rain join in the strain,
　And louder their murmurs grow :
　　" Nay, Mortal, nay,
　　For your soul would stay
Bound down in the depths below.
No more then above, your own true Love,
　Might you hope again to see,
　　If from earth's hard fight,
　　With impious flight,
　Like a coward you should flee."

Then I pause and cry :　" O God, on high !
　What can I do with my life ?
　　For I scarce can live,
　　And I may not die,
I'm worn and weary with strife.
And the waves' refrain rings in my brain,
　As heedless they sound their lay :
　　" No more shall ye meet,
　　And your loved one greet,
So go on your dreary way."

But while I thus cry to God on high,
　Yet another sound breaks in ;
　　It is soft and low,
　　And still, even so,
'Tis heard o'er the wild waves' din.
And I raise my head with sudden hope,

As the Christmas bells I hear,
   And sweet and slow,
   On my heart's deep woe,
They whisper their words of cheer.

" Mortal, not so, on your sad path go,
   With a proud, firm step, and free ;
    Trust yourself to God,
    Take the path He trod,
Then shall you your loved one see."
So hope came back to me once again
   And I bowed my head, and prayed ;
    I minded no more
    The waves on the shore,
For my longing soul was stayed.

.   .   .   .   .

Yes, ye shall meet, to part no more, for ever ;
Hope on, strive on, give way to grief no more !
God does not mean your faithful hearts to sever,
Your Love in safety waits you on Heav'n's shore.
C. CHALMERS.

The Sun-Bright Clime!

Have ye heard, have ye heard, of that sun-bright clime,
Unstain'd by sorrow, unhurt by time,
Where age hath no power o'er the fadeless frame,
Where the eye is fire, and the heart is flame—
  Have ye heard of that sun-bright clime?
There are rivers of water gushing there,
'Mid blossoms of beauty, strangely fair;
And a thousand wings are hovering o'er
The dazzling wave and the golden shore—
  They are found in that sun-bright clime.
There is the City whose name is Light,
With the diamond's ray and the ruby bright;
And ensigns are waving, and banners unfurl,
Over walls of jasper and gates of pearl
  That are fixed in that sun-bright clime.
There are myriads of forms arrayed in white,
Beings of beauty clothed in Light;
They dwell in their own immortal bowers,
Mid the fadeless hues of countless flowers
  That spring in that sun-bright clime.
Ear hath not heard, eye hath not seen,
Its swelling songs or its changeless sheen
For the vests of Light, and harps of gold,
And crowns of glory, wax not old
  Or fade in that sun-bright clime.
But far away is this sinless clime,
Unstain'd by sorrow, unhurt by time;
Where amid all things most fair is given
The home of the just, and its name is Heaven—
  The name of that sun-bright clime!

       Margaret Campbell.

Autumn

Homeward the swallows fly,
Leaves fade, and fall, and die—
          Autumn is nigh.

" Across a narrow sea "—
Joyous the thought must be—
          " The skies are blue."

Life's summertime is o'er:
Unto a sunlit shore
          My soul looks forth,

Prepared to take its flight
When faith is lost in sight,
          In realms of Light ;

For there my loved ones stand,
A white-robed, happy band.
          Awaiting me.

                    KATHERINE CHARTERS.

The First Easter Morning

In a beautiful garden, at earliest dawn,
A woman stood weeping, that first Easter Morn;
A dearly-loved Friend had been from her torn,
     Three days ago.

In His grave an angel sat at the head,
Who, when he beheld her, tenderly said,
" Why seek ye the living among the dead?
     Why weepest thou?

" I know ye seek Jesus: He is not here—
He told thee, in Galilee, He'd re-appear:
Go, tell His disciples, and Peter, so dear,
     He has risen."

She turned her about, this bidding to do—
How could she believe it? could it be true?
Then, through misty tears, appeared to her view,
     Her risen Lord.

Thinking He was the gardener, she hasten'd to say,
" Oh, Sir, tell me, have you borne Him away?
Tell me, oh, tell me, where now He doth lay,
     That I may go."

He spake but one word—He breathed her own name!
Then joy to her stricken heart quickly there came,
And she would have clasped His pierced hand just the
   same
     As in Galilee.

" Touch me not ! " He said kindly, then gently with-
    drew :
But He gave her something for Him to do—
" Go, tell my disciples, and Peter, too,
      I am risen."

Yes, Christ, He has risen and gone up above,
And pleads with His Father with infinite love
For all His disciples who still on earth rove,
      Hallelujah !
               GEORGIANNA THIRZA CHILD
                       (*Blind*).

'Tis a Good World

When Summer clothes the trees anew,
And woods are decked with myriad flowers,
When play, and dance and song with you
Joyously fill the golden hours,
    'Tis a good world.

When Autumn turns the trees to gold
And woods take on a russet hue,
Tho' skies are grey, and evenings cold,
When riding o'er the downs with you,
    'Tis a good world.

When Winter makes the branches bare,
And woods are coverts from the storm,
If o'er the meadows bounds the hare,
And hills are echoing the horn,
    'Tis a good world.
               BLANCHE CARDEN.

Romance-Time

Rain comes in April,
    And June brings the Rose;
But Lilac-time is Romance-time—
    Ask anyone who knows!
                RUTH V. COONLEY.

Colour

I see the sunset through the trees—
    Its burnished gold is thrilling me;
And through the green and leafy boughs—
    My soul responds in ecstasy.
                RUTH V. COONLEY.

The Wind

The Wind is a Lover. No one can discover
His unseen caresses that cover her being,
    While passing above her.
She thrills at his touch, as he tries to uncover
Her beautiful body which calls him to love her.
His passionate breezes around her still hover—
The Wind is a jealous, delectable Lover!
                RUTH V. COONLEY.

A Sunset in Simla

See how the golden ball doth sink
  Into the darkish, bluish west !
See how it wanes, and then doth blink,
  While it so slowly comes to rest,
With streaks of fiery red
On a bluish-purplish bed
Of clouds and vapours dark,
Behind the hills which mark
The bounds of Simla, green !
There's a streak of light,
So red and blue and white,
And yet so fair and sheen,
It glimmers through the mountain-screen.

But soon the glimmering light
Grows dim, and then goes out.
And new lights start to gleam in sight
From a thousand lamps that shine,
Tier, over tier, in a line,
From houses drenched in rain.
And poor pedestrians plod in pain,
To reach a club or home,
Under a bluish-blackish dome
Of a threat'ning sky and a torrent of rain.

                                N. C. DARNWALLA.

Necessity

And what art thou,
      Necessity?
Hast thou no law,
      Necessity?
When thou dost make us bow
To thine own-made law,
Dost thou e'er care a straw
      For our necessity?

Art thou, indeed, a mother
      Of discovery,
And inventions made by man,
      Oh, Necessity?
Or art thou just a brother
      Of Tyranny,
Driving like a slave-driver,
      As the Devil only can?

And dost thou not lay
Low many on the way,
Who die as thy prey,
      Grim Necessity?

Dost thou keep statistics true,
      Necessity?
Then say, in number who are more
'Mong those who fought their way—
How many swam to shore,
      Necessity?

And how many of the brave
Found a watery grave?
How many fell a prey
To thy tyrant sway,
    Without Pity,
    Fell Necessity?

        N. C. DARNWALLA.

The Country Cottage

I see an old thatched cottage
  On a sunny hill ·
A door, two little windows,
  Walls with ivy frill.

Drowned in a flood of colours,
  Grass and leafy trees,
And flowers that are counted
  By the droning bees.

I hear the thrush and goldfinch
  In the bushes, nigh,
And other birds are dancing
  On the branches by.

I smell the healthy fragrance
  Though in towns I roam:
Heaven dwells within me
  When I dream of home.

        ELIAS DAVIES.

Lost Enchantment

O World of Mist,
O Land of Heart's Desire,
Where once I dwelt;
O Shadow-Land,
O, Isle of Happy Laughter,
Fare thee well!
Some uncouth hand,
Some rude, untutored mail
Of infidel,
Has torn the veil
Of many hours close weaving,
Where I wrapped
My inmost heart.
The fragrance of the pine-trees
There captured was;
The sad lost star
Fast meshed in weed-grown lake
Of twilight purple.
　　　　And now it lies
Cross-rent, and darkly sullied,
At my lost feet.
And the fair land,
The Isle of Happy Laughter,
Vanished is,
Like subtle bloom
That's brushed from purple berries
By her soft lips.
And here I stand
All naked, cold, and wind-buffed,
In a strange land.

J. DAVISON.

" Black Magic "

Go you into the forest,
And wade in the swamps, to your knees,
Where the amber flowers
Of the Indian fruit
Glint under the cinnamon-trees.
Pick of the un-named magic,
But wait till the moon is high :
Taste only then, for, if before,
The natives say you die !
And who can tell what you shall know
When you sink in swooning sleep ?
For on awaking you must laugh,
But also you must weep.

                    KAYE DRUMMOND.

The Mills of God

The Mills of God are grinding,
Grinding slow, but sure ;
    The Mills of God are grinding
    For the rich, and for the poor.

No use is it for one to say
That So-and-So has more than I :
    No use at all is it to say
    That So-and-So is worse than I.

For those who have ten talents
That much will be required of them ;
    And those who e'en two talents have,
    Must render full account of them.

All ye who understanding have,
Bear well these words in mind—
    All ye who understanding have
    " Seek well, and ye shall find."

Yet do not seek too far afield,
Look, first, quite near to home;
    Nay, do not seek too far afield—
    There is no need to roam.

We are *not* " Puppets," as some say,
Of a hard or cruel " Fate " ;
    We are *not* " Puppets," as some say,
    But we (most of us) " learn "—*too late* !

Full many a gay and rollicking song
Hits out both straight and true ;
    Full many a merely " Comic " song
    Bears a " hint " for me *and* you.

                 M. DAUBENY.

Rejected

" Cheer up, old pal,"
    Says Joe to me,
" There are more fish
    Inside the sea."

There are more fish,
    Well do I know ;
But all the bait
    Has finished, Joe.

                ELIAS DAVIES.

The Night Wind

Softly, softly whispering,
  Through the weeping firs,
A little lonely wind at night,
  Sadly sighing, stirs.

All the world is sleeping,
  All asleep, save I,
Wandering o'er the mountain-side—
  A weary lullaby.

Down the valleys wandering,
  Love-lorn, all alone,
Seeking, but to no avail—
  Oh, whither has she gone?

Whither, whither, wandering,
  Across the Western sea?
White wings, ever wheeling,
  Carry word for me.

Say, I walk on sunless shores,
  By sullen, angry waves,
Alone, and sadly greeting,
  Amongst the lost ships' graves.

Each day is like the rolling tides
  That slowly ebb and flow,
An age succeeding yesterday,
  And ever one to follow.

J. S. LL. DOCKAR-DRYSDALE.

My Dream

In a cottage, peacefully sleeping,
I had a most beautiful dream.
A soul had passed beyond keeping—
Oh, how 'twas changed ! to earth unreal !—
And while I was silently watching,
A most beautiful form was revealed.

And, oh, what exquisite beauty
Came gliding through space to me !
As my arms went out to receive her,
She turned her fair face to see—
" Jesus—Look !—is there and is waiting,
With music and angels, for me."

Oh, beauteous spirit, divinely pure
With heavenly azure we all adore,
Wafting a message from shore to shore !
In a quick'ning moment how changed we'll be !
From sin and sorrow then set free,
Our earthly bodies no more we'll see.

What a delightful picture,
When our eyes are opened to see
The beauty that's all surpassing !—
And memories linger, ah, me !—
Oh, Jesus, that great Designer
Of heaven and earth and sea !

In the clouds a beautiful opening,
So bright my eyes could not see ;
But I knew there was something lovely,
With peaceful surroundings, near me :
And, oh, what a wonderful story
Was revealed in a dream to me !

Jesus says to one and all,
" I am your redeemer."

MARY E. BENINGTON.

My Garden

Stream-kissed she wakes, and birds chant rhapsodies
    In praise of her, for on her cool, glad face
    The Kingfisher and Moor-hen find a place
To nest them, confident that no man sees ;
There, panniers pollen-laden, come wild Bees,
    And Dragon-flies ; and there, in close embrace,
    Green lawns and silver waters interlace
To make her fair—this shrine of memories.

And soon, 'mid lessening fragrance, one by one,
    Sweet briars and bergamot—her pensioners—go ;
    Then, on each bush, the frail, silk gossamers show
Their frosted threads, till, dreaming in the sun,
    And safe beneath the coverlet of snow,
She sleeps, my garden—white as cloistered Nun.
                        KATE ELLISON.

A Sonnet to the Unknown Warrior

November 11th.

Remote, you lie, beneath your wreaths of bay,
    And by your silence all the hopes defeat
    Of those who claim you now. No quickening beat
Of heart can make you answer when we say,
" What of your childhood? where your boyish play
    And which of us has passed you in the street,
    Or held your hand in greeting, heard your feet
Go by us as you hurried on your way? "

And in your dreams before you came to die,
    Had you no prescience of that wondrous fate—
    Loud challenge to a silent Laureate—
Which brought you back in death to occupy
A place unparalleled in history?
    Unknown ! Yet known to all the world too late !
                      KATE ELLISON.

The Cloud

Across the sky a dark cloud raced,
Over the sand its shadow traced,
Turning the blue sea into green,
Casting a gloom on the pools unseen.
Meadows of buttercups, pale-green trees
Darkened and shivered. Restless as these,
Joyful young children, at play in the hay,
Watched till the cloud had blown away.

Cats on the sills opened their eyes,
Aware of the chill, and hundreds of flies
Ceased their drowsy drone on the pane,
Only to start it again and again.
A blind man lifted his sightless eyes,
Feeling, not seeing, the cloud in the skies
A dragon-fly spread her shimmering wings,
And trembled because of unseen things.

Hurrying to work, a city girl heard,
In the shadowed garden, the note of a bird :
A stream in the hills was clear and cold—
Just for a moment the world was old.
Just for a moment, then the cloud past !
Free'd from the gloom the cloud had cast,
Quickened and rich, suffused with light,
A wave in its blueness turned suddenly white
As it finally lapped on the golden sand ;
An infant chuckled and stretched out her hand ;
The mother blessed her dear little one :
A shadow had darkened the light of the sun.
                              ·· Wilna E. R. Fairley.

Come Nigh To Him

Come nigh unto the Saviour now,
   And to Him all your cares express ;
When thus your head you meekly bow,
   He soon will all your cares suppress.

Speak low—He hears what you would say !
   Just bow, in reverence, the knee :
He will not from you turn away—
   He gently calls, " Come Unto Me."

Though daily frets will sometimes sever
   An earthly friend (for a short while),
Just rest upon His " Great Endeavour "—
   He is your Friend, and bids you smile.

If by some foolish fault you err,
   And you, your friends misunderstand,
With vain regrets your mind you stir—
   He knows, and He will by you stand.

The word or action oft misplaced
   By ignorance or want of thought—
He knows the fault; your need He traced,
   And with His life your peace He bought.

Ah, precious thought of God, to send
   His Son, a willing sacrifice !
In simple faith on Him depend,
   For you " He gladly paid the price."

He is your true and dearest Friend,
　He will not you misunderstand,
If to His promise you attend,
　And by the right you firmly stand.

So let not cares or worldly strife
　Disturb the peace He came to bring,
But trust Him in your daily life,
　With heart and mind His praises sing.

C. FARR.

A Soliloquy

Oh, Solitude, that gives me time
To think of all God's gifts awhile :
Of friendships, and good times to be.
Of golden hours beside the sea,
Of glorious sunshine, birds and flowers,
Of rippling brooks and shady bowers—
The things He gives to me.

When in the busy towns I stay,
These blessings seem to fade away :
I only see the hurrying throng,
And quite forget the wild bird's song ;
I only hear the rush of things,
Forgetting how the swallow flings
His song into the sky.

Dear Solitude, that gives me eyes
To see the beauty 'neath God's skies !
I feel the wind blow care away ;
And know well that in God's own day
My wants will all be satisfied,
My sadness all be rectified,
Peace come to stay.

TRUDY FENTON.

My Dog

You came to me in puppy days,
A little toddling mite;
You suffered all a puppy's ills,
Through day and endless night.

Your little bed was lonely,
Your pals were far away;
Through the long, dark, dreary night you sat,
Whining for the day.

I wonder, will folks ever know
What's in a doggie's mind,
When orders come for him to go,
And leave his home behind,

To face, perhaps, a future hard,
A home with no kind word,
Where faithful duty oft is robbed
Of duty's just reward?

You have that grand old quality
That most human natures lack—
Fidelity! that noble charm,
Bred in a noble pack,

Whether 'tis on the mountain top,
Or in the sunny dale
Whether the night turns rough and dark,
Or the wind becomes a gale

O Faithful One, thou'rt ever near,
To cheer me on my way,
And by your noble actions speak
The words you cannot say.

Who can resist those pleading eyes,
Pleading for homely care?
God grant that all who have a dog,
Will hear a doggie's prayer!

VIOLET A. FENTON.

Life's River

Sometimes I feel so happy,
    I could sing upon Life's way;
Sometimes I want to tarry,
    And let misery hold its sway.

One day I soar up skywards,
    One day I reach the depths;
One day I'm looking forward,
    The next day I regret.

Like the ever-swelling water,
    Life races on a-pace;
The thing's that really matter,
    I hardly like to face.

Just like the rushing water,
    We ne'er in one place stay;
We rise and fall and falter
    On our Life's long Highway.

QUEENIE M. FISHER.

Hope for a Discouraged Life

For somewhere a Soul keeps yearning
    For a song that might have been,
Sung from the pages of Destiny,
    Wrapped in a tissue of Dreams :
And a light that failed, would be born again,
    And a heart would laugh with Peace
For Joy would whisper to Courage, " Remain ! "
    And all misdoubtings cease.

For a veil was drawn over laughter,
    And a heart was steeped in sighs,
To burn with the hope of Hereafter
    That lies beyond the skies ;
For 'tis only the Music of Heaven,
    The certainty of Childhood's Land,
That may raise the Soul from Darkness,
    To Shine on Security's Stand.

                              MARY FORTE.

Beauty

There's beauty in a noble tree,
   And in a lock of hair;
It cloaks itself in modesty
   To catch you, unaware.

There's beauty in the western sky
   A-flame with sunset glow;
Though many a casual passer-by
   Won't lift his eyes to know.

And there's a kind of restlessness
   That beauty brings about,
That leaves the vaguest breathlessness,
   Like snowdrops coming out.

There's beauty in a ship at sea,
   Which lingers in her sail;
And in the dawn-light o'er the lea
   When all the East grows pale.

There's beauty in a swallow's wings,
   And in a woman's hand;
Oh, beauty lies in everything,
   If we could understand.

NANCY GEORGE.

Amerdale in Winter

The mountains, black, are streaked with snow,
And gusts of sleet and hail
Fall on the slopes and screes below—
And this is Amerdale.

By low stone walls on every side,
The pastures are surrounded ;
No cattle feeding in them now,
No bells on sheep are sounded.

The rushing becks come foaming down,
The Fosse is in full spate,
Its pebbles whirled and swirled and dirled—
A most tumultuous state.

One road leads through to Halton Ghyll—
Above, the skies are grey;
And with bent head, and blue with cold,
The postman ploughs his way.

But sheltered under Belder's side,
And standing in its garth,
A solid, white farm-house appears—
Ah, here is home and hearth !

KATE GILBERT.

Rosemary in Shadow

" One who has suffered " would understand
And give us a warm and a loving hand ;
" One who has suffered " would feel right well
The deeps of a sorrow too sad to tell.

" One who has suffered " would know the " Why ? "
Of a trembling lip and a smothered sigh ;
All the ache of the heart, and the wistful eye,
That " Someone " sees, Who is ever nigh.

For " One who has suffered " the low, low bell
And the ivied wreath, and the organ knell,
And the silent room, and the lonely stair,
And the dead, dead pen, and the vacant chair—

Oh, shadowed morning, and dreary night !
Oh, the long lone trail, and the tearless fight !
Yes, " One who has suffered " would understand,
And give us a true and a kindly hand.

" One who has suffered " is wise in " sight "
With the knowledge born of that Inner Light ;
Sees the rough steep path we must tread alone,
Where the storms beat high, and the flowers lie prone
In the Garden of Love that we once have known.

When the sun dips low in a misty shroud,
And Love's Star is lost in a darkened cloud,
Ah ! " One who has suffered " will understand,
And give the dear clasp of a friendly hand.

ALYS R. GILES.

The Tragedy of War

Thousands of thousands went out to die, thousands
    of thousands fell;
A tragedy scarring the earth's fair face, a blight and a
    slur on the human race,
       A tragedy without peer.
Yet when the cry, " We're at war ! " rang out, that
    cry was acclaimed by a joyful shout
       From the throats of our men and boys.
All those who saw it, will never forget the sight of
    London that night
Lord, grant that we may never again be faced with so
    awful a sight—
The sight of a populace turning wild in the lust for blood
    and death,
The throwing away of youth and life, the needless
    sorrow and endless strife,
       The giving of their last breath !

     .   .   .   .   .

You men of Great Britain, remember, your Empire
    stands for Peace !
Fight in your hearts for her glory, that her name may
    never cease
To be loved, respected and honoured by nations
    throughout the world,
Because you, the men of her Empire, have supported
    her Flag, unfurled.
Remember, oh, Youth of England, we call on you to
    uphold
The wonderful name of your nation, which cannot be
 priced in gold.
                    PATRICIA H. GILLON.

The Easiest Way ?

A mind's struggle against the temptation to commit suicide, when faced with failure and disgrace.

Icy fingers clutched at my heart-strings, terror troubled
    my brain ;
I flung myself down by the waterside, numbed and
    deadened with pain.
Something rose up of the darkness before me—some
    thing, I know not what :
An arm, stretched out, and beckoned, to call me away
    from that fatal spot.

A strong hand fell on my shoulder; a voice hushed by
    the breeze—
The moon in her eery splendour, was caressing the
    rustling trees.
The voice of that great stillness fell as music upon my
    soul ;
My wounded heart was mended, my shattered spirit
    whole.

" Others besides you have suffered; others have
    struggled and failed;
Yet you looked around in the shadows for the easiest
    way and you hailed
The fallen angel of sinners, to show you the road to
    Heaven !
You would fling in the face of the Giver, the wonderful
    gift He has given !

" Rise! Gather strength from the darkness; gather
    joy and light from the day ;
Help others who suffer unduly, to gaze through the
    mists on their way ;
To pick out from the shadows the sunshine, to conquer
    with smiles each sigh.
Do you wish to be branded a coward ? " " I do not,"
    answered I.

PATRICIA H. GILLON.

Alone

Against the pale of evening sky,
The elm-trees reared black heads of filigree
The smoke-blue shadows of the wood
Ran up the hill to where the sun,
With faintly orange finger-tips,
Had smeared the brow with gold.
I stood alone.
The air was still, and a quiet peace
Stole into the numbness of my aching soul;
But you had gone. . . .

NANCY GEORGE.

Parted

'Tis love that lingers in my heart,
   A love for you, so true :
I often dreamt we'd never part—
   I ne'er would have from you.

But Fate has led us two apart,
   The which I mourn to-day;
My constant thoughts for you, Sweetheart,
   With memories fondly play.

Red roses in the garden, Love,
   Are waiting your return;
Your night-bird carols its sweet songs—
   Oh, how my heart doth burn !

The river flows so swiftly by,
   While on the stoep I pray,
Awaiting your return, Dear Heart,
   Still watching day by day.

Oh, I am lone while we're apart,
   My soul for you doth yearn ;
There's naught in all the world, dear Love,
   For me, but your return.

But as I watch yon setting sun,
   Its last rays seem to say,
To mend my heart you will come back,
   And stay with me for aye.

LOVICH GOORDEEN,

Happiness

There's happiness in the smile on a loved one's face;
There's happiness in the shape of a flower;
The rippling flow of a brook adds another drop;
The glimpse of a sunset from a mountain-top
Thrills us and fills us with delicious delight,
For nature in all her moods is ever bright,
With truth and sincerity her only light.
To some, the flowers, to others, a child's caress,
Convey a feeling, deep, of blessedness.
For all our dreams to come true, is less than possible,
But at least a few we are destined to realize.
Not to despise our friends; to abhor lies;
To cling to the noble and the true;
To be open-hearted, courageous, and loving, too;
To look for happiness in caring for others,
Their welfare and their interests—
In all these things lies happiness.

BESSIE GRUNDY.

Ver Perpetuum

I dreamed last night
  That the leaves were falling:
And when I went forth in the morning light
  They were falling about my head;
    They were falling,
  Cold and dead.

O Life, thy years
  Fade as the leaves are fading;
And, sapped by the cold world's cares and fears,
  Like a burden man bears them on
    Still, still fading,
  Chill and wan.

But there is gold
  In the leaves that are dying,
In the withered face of the leaves so old;
  Promise that where they cling,
    Dying, dying,
  Flowers will spring.

C. W. GRIFFIN.

Two Gardens

Suggested by a visit to the Royal Cripples Hospital, Northfield.

I walked in a beautiful garden. The peace of Heaven
    was there—
The lilies, the roses and the sweet mignonette, all spoke
    of the Master's care ;
The birds as they flitted around me, seemed trying to
    tell of His love :
Oh ! 'twas good to be there in that garden fair, 'neath
    the bright blue sky above.

Just close to that self-same garden (there was only a
    pathway between)
Was one whose beds were filled with flowers, which
    differed from those I'd just seen.
'Twas as tho', when in bud, they'd been blighted by
    a cold wind or lack of the sun,
For those frail little blossoms had needed more care
    than the hardier ones had done.

From whence comes the power that has reached them ?
See ! they're lifting their heads toward the sun :
    Tender hands, loving hearts, now surround them,
    And " Love's " healing work has begun.
Oh ! you who have " flower-filled " gardens,
    Which are sheltered and warmed by the sun,
Pray remember there's one of God's gardens,
    Needs the help of us all, everyone.

Ellen M. Gibson.

Be Still

Stoop and drink ; and in that drinking know
  That you will stir the waters of clear thinking.
Look down ; and every grain of sand will show
  Unrippled, still, until .the act of drinking
Wakes the lip-touched waters into waves that flow
Out, and around, to stir the sleeping sands below.

Be still ! For every act unpremeditated,
  Flings a pebble into Life's still Pool ;
And dead desires, lying there, unsated,
  Rise to confound the simple fool
Who dares disturb the rest so long awaited
By hope, for things that yet are uncreated.
    Be still ! O be still !

N. E. GILMORE.

Musings

Life—and death ; great matters these, with much
    between ;
Two great adventures—the Seen and the Unseen :
Life lived, and loved, that proudly bears
Brave banners high ; and death that dares
To prove that love, and that God cares.
His Love ? The sunlight, flowers and trees,
The quiet woods, and shadow'd evening breeze,
And little children. After these——
Comes death, hand-in-hand with Ease.
And so we know
The way that He would have us go.

. N. E. GILMORE.

The Dahlias are Drooping

The dahlias are drooping . . .
Autumn has walked my garden
                                    and stooping,
touched the flowers with sleep.
    Even the woods beyond begin to weep:
their leafy glory takes its golden way
to dust; and bare limbs gaunt and gray
are stretched upon an Autumn sky
that glows with a deep sunset fire—
the Phoenix-pyre
                of Summer.
    Driven from this changing scene,
the frightened swallows fast are flying:
and the quiet evening air is stirred
by the strange, distant crying
                                of a bird.
    The groping dusk has found my garden;
and in dim shadow-shrouds,
the dahlias are disappearing . . .

                                SIDNEY GRAY.

The Call of the Sunset

I saw a Sunset linger,
and enthralled,
stood watching till it seemed the finger
of the Lord stopped painting, and began
to beckon.
Over the silence the Sunset called,
but Fear stole the heart of me,
swept every part of me,
so that I ran . . .
                 on and on.
Once I half-turned,
but behold ! though the heavens still burned
with the glory of God . . . God was gone.
SIDNEY GRAY.

Turmoil

Can anything on earth bring peace to me,
Beyond a moment's respite from the strife
Of torn desires, ambitions—bring the key
Of living, make this so far wasted life
Of worth—that something may be given back
For all the things that falsely I have claimed,
Have grasped so firmly, but which now do lack
The glamour I had hoped for, and lie maimed?
If death alone can soothe my troubled state,
Let death come swiftly; or if still there be
Behind this mask of fire and love and hate
Some spark of truth, some glow that yet is me,
May I be quick to kindle it to flame,
And stir emotions shall be worth the name.

BETTY A. GARDNER.

November Nights

How good it is to be at home
On nights like these,
When, outside, raw November winds
Rush madly through the trees,

Tearing the last remaining leaves
From every limb,
Whirling them high in spiral dance
As o'er the ground they skim ;

And, drenching town and countryside,
Cold, relentless rain
Beats in ceaseless monotony
On every window pane !

Inside the room the fire burns bright,
The lamp glows warm.
The atmosphere of peace and calm,
In contrast to the storm,

Bathes the tired body, the weary mind,
In sleepless dreams.
Sweet hours of rest, in close proximity
To one whose presence means

More than the heart can e'er express
In mortal words !
We do not speak, there is no need—
The intimate silence affords

Closer communion of mind and soul
Than peace can give :
We gaze into each other's eyes,
And in each other live.

RICHARD GREY.

Mummy's Lullaby

Go to sleep, my darling !
Flowers and birds their heads now bow to rest ;
Rock thou to sleep with them,
Upon your mummy's breast. ᛜ
In the blue sky the glowing moon is nigh,
Her beams peer at your face in silent wonder ;
While night wind blows, your pleasant dream still grows,
And twinkle all the stars on your sweet slumber.
Thy mind is now with elves in Fairyland ;
An angel o'er thy cot his wings has spread,
To guard my pretty one, the long night through,
Until the day-break rouse thee once again.

JOHN O. JOSE.

Meeting

Courage and wistful yearning
  Mischief and slight surprise,
Are strange unused companions
  Of oddly assorted size :
And stranger still when they all peep forth
  From a pair of beautiful eyes.

They said, in their starry language,
  That they sought for a chance to smile,
And I felt as I read their message,
  A longing to taste their guile ;
For is it not well for a man to walk
  In Paradise for a while ?

It was on the high seas in autumn,
  When life was an easy thing,
When many a scudding cloudlet
  Was having a gladsome fling,
And the mists that deaden the questing soul
  Had parted and taken wing.

We scaled o'er the walls of silence
  With the ease of a child as it plays ;
And oh ! what a world of sweetness
  Was spread for my wondering gaze !
But I knew that refreshed with this rare delight,
  We would sunder and go our ways.

We would sunder and leave no traces,
　　Like ships that pass in the night :
Yet ships in their passing tremble,
　　Tremble and show a light—
Ah ! would that my spirit could fathom the dark
　　And read me the signs outright !

A. HAWKINS.

Something to cheer Us

Let's be glad of the earth beneath ;
Let's be glad of the sky above,
Of flowers that grow, of birds that sing,
And of Heaven, and a Father's love !

Oh, it matters not how young we are,
Or e'en how old we have grown to be,
Some blessings remain to constantly cheer,
The path of you and me.

And it matters not where we may dwell,
In wintry climes, or fair,
Something is there, to cheer and to tell
Of God and His loving care.

Though clouds may gather and shadows fall
Across your path and mine,
When we come through, as we always do,
We find that the sun can shine.

I'm glad God made us all much alike,
With the same sort of world to live in ;
And to all who believe, I'm glad He gave
The hope of a home in Heaven.

And although we cannot be sure
Of what wrong and evil may do,
I'm glad there is nothing destroyed,
But what His Hand can renew ;

And although they seek to do their worst
With sword, and tongue, and pen,
When they have finished, I'm glad, aren't you,
That God can all renew again?

So be glad of the earth beneath;
And be glad of the sky above,
Of flowers that grow, and birds that sing,
And of Heaven, and a Father's love!

C. HAYSOM.

Plea at Evening to Mother

When brown leaves rustle through the empty park
Like grim reminders of the passing years,
Remorse arises in my aching heart,
That I have often filled thine eyes with tears.
Forgive the errors of the bygone days;
And may thy loving soul remain at peace
Beneath the setting sun's becalming rays
That in life's Autumn gently bring release
From strife. The burdens of the past thou bore
With patience, and with undimmed fortitude:
My love, I swear, is thine for ever more,
My loyalty and deepest gratitude.
So may a quiet rapture fill thy breast
Now that we face the secret night of rest.

WILLIAM P. HEROD, M.A., Yale University.

The Sacred Lake

There is a strange and placid sacred lake
Amidst the mystic peaks of quietude,
Where tranquil, lost souls nevermore awake,
Are rapt in dreams of magic solitude.
And there they drift as shrouds of mist at eve,
Filtering through the drooping lilies' scent.
Below the clouds of all the souls that grieve,
They faintly hear the silvery teardrops spent.
The tired spirits breathe the opiate air
Under the Aegis of the Buddha's smile.
The wraiths of Yogis wander freely there,
In breezes blending with their sleep the while :
Ah ! there is known the blessed calm of death,
Mingled within the scarcely taken breath.

WILLIAM PIRTLE HEROD, M.A., Yale University.

To a Child

Dearest ! thou art the month of May.
  In thee I seem to see
Fair apple blossom on the spray,
  Or anemone.

There is some secret sweet within thine eyes,
  Which calls to me ;
Beneath the shell-like lids it lies,
  The heart of thee.

CAPEL HALL.

Rapture

There is ecstasy in living
On waking in the Spring,
And love and laughter in the heart
That make the pulses sing.

Oh, the mist upon the mountains,
The foam upon the sea,
And the golden glint of sunshine
Fine rapture bring to me !

'Tis the wind among the pine-trees,
The green upon the lea,
That gladsome look of promise give
Of summer soon to be.

For 'tis youth is in the Springtime,
And freedom from all care,
Ever constant looking forward,
A hope without despair.

CAPEL HALL.

Birth

Oh ! exquisite the pale translucent dawn,
Arrayed in garb of amethyst and gold
She doth with close embrace the earth enfold,
And thus the glad triumphant day is born.

Enchanting is the coming of the spring,
As if the wind had rent dark winter's screen
And with soft breath girt all the world in green,
Bearing her offspring on the new year's wing.

CAPEL HALL.

In the Twilight

Round the fireside, in the twilight,
　Comes a throng of phantom faces ;
And the past comes back before me
　As I range them in their places.

Faces of my early childhood ;
　Faces of the long departed ;
Friends of boyhood, youth's dear comrades,
　Staunch and true, and loyal-hearted.

And they seem to hover near me,
　Happy memories recalling,
As I sit and muse at twilight,
　When the evening shades are falling.

One bright face comes in the twilight,
  With its deep-blue eyes of beauty :
This face was my inspiration
  Through life's cares, and toil, and duty.

In those eyes, serene and tender,
  Her great soul shone, constant ever ;
Cheering, helping, leading onward,
  Strengthening me in each endeavour.

Long we trod life's path together—
  Now she lives in memory only ;
And I sit alone at twilight—
  She is gone, and I am lonely.

Other forms come back to memory
  In the twilight's waking dream,
But amid that throng of faces
  This sweet face stands out supreme.

Round the fireside, in the twilight,
  Comes that throng of phantom faces ;
All my life comes back before me
  While I range them in their places.

CLAIRE INGLEDEW.

"Laddie"

We had such fun together,
　My little dog and I,
In every kind of weather,
　Hot, cold, wet or dry.

I never had to coax him—
　He was ready any time,
To romp, and tear, and scamper
　(He's two, and I am nine.)

There isn't a squirrel or rabbit
　That Laddie and I haven't found;
For we've searched every nook and corner
　For miles and miles around.

And once, when he was a puppy,
　He chewed up Dad's Sunday hat;
And that night, when no one was watching,
　He ate off the end of the mat.

'N Mother said, "That dog's a nuisance!"
　'N Dad growled, "He's just a pest!"
But in spite of whatever *they* call him,
　I know he's the pick of the best.

And I love every hair of his body,
　From his head to his muddy, white paws,
'Cause he came to me one winter
　As a gift—straight from Santa Claus.

G´

Now, his collar hangs there with its dog-tag,
His empty plate's down by the shed;
And his—Oh, I can't stand it no longer!
Laddie—my playmate—is dead!

GLADYS LUCK HALL.

To ——

Like a lamp that's set in some high window,
Making weary wanderers think of home—
Like one shining star amid the darkness,
Brightening all the path of those who roam—
Like the air of some new-born Spring morning,
Full of uplift, joy, vitality—
Like a handclasp, strong, and firm and tender,
When o'erwhelmed by Life's finality—
Like the mist which veils a summer dawning,
Adding beauty to each field and tree.
Like all these, and, oh, much more besides them,
The thought of your dear friendship is to me.

FANNY L. ILES.

The Rush-bearing

Long years ago, with Summer's ending,
In the sweet old days of England,
Our chuich floors were strewn with rushes,
Ready for September's harvest,
Gathered near the river, winding,
Clear and cool, along the valley,
Winding, winding, ever winding,
Flowing onward to the ocean :
Yearly was a day appointed,
Set for gathering the rushes.
In the happiness of their hearts,
Youths and maidens their troth plighted,
Neither of them then remembering
Times when they knew not the other.
Still is kept this festival ;
Our workers still go forth to seek
A holiday, so long desired,
Earned through a year of faithful toil
For their homes and little ones,
And the welfare of their country.
It is a wondrous exodus !
Thousands of thousands go afar,
Seeking change and recreation.
Still their troth plight youths and maidens,
As in the days of long ago :
Youth oft seeks another maiden,
Not the dear one of his childhood.

M. E. Hirst.

Not Only

We praise Thee for the harvest, Lord!
    The fields of rustling corn
Are symbols of Thy never-failing grace to man,
Reminding us that for Thy children Thou dost plan
    Each night and morn.

Not only for the harvest, Lord,
    Do we present our praise,
But also for the loveliness that round us gleams—
The flame of scarlet flowers, the sunshine's gilded
    beams,
    And starlight's jewelled blaze.

But help us, Lord, not only to
    Adore when skies are fair;
But should the sunlight fade, and clouds obscure
    our day,
Oh, help us then, tho' hard, to praise Thee for the
    grey,
    And feel Thy presence there.

                  G. ERIC HODGINS.

Goodwood, June 8th, 1934

Cloud Pageants overwhelmed me, as I stepped from
    day to twilight.
These quiet woods, as yet unmarred by modern
    Philistine,
Lay basking in the shades of long ago.
No sound of woodman's axe, no clearing vile,
Announced the passing of a heritage
Which fast is mouldering.
As yet unmarred : nature pursued her course,
      This calm June evening,
      Uninterrupted.
A cuckoo's note, a ring-dove's wistful coo,
A pheasant's harsh cok-cok,
All muffled by the leafy foliage,
Breathed out contentment.
Ah, how long will all this loveliness
Remain unspoiled ?
If poverty is powerless, then soon shall Desolation
Ravish these solitudes, and make of them
      A sprawling mushroom-growth of modern dwell-
        ings.
If hopes and prayers are riches, our descendants
Will yet admire the mysteries
Of this, our Fairyland.

                   E. E. HUGHES-HUGHES.

My Windows

Give me a window facing east,
Where I may watch the sun's uprising,
And wonder what the new-born day
Will hold for my surprising.

One room must face the sunny south,
That, even when he hoards his treasure,
Some portion of the sun-god's gold
Perchance may overflow his measure.

But I must have a north room, too,
That when the summer's heat oppresses,
I may escape and rest awhile
From that same sun's too fierce caresses.

But if I am denied all these,
Just give me one where I may linger
To see, each eve, the homing sun
Caress the earth with loving finger ;

To see that touch make, unaware,
A beauty more than tongue can tell ;
To say at each day's glorious end,
" Day, we have been good friends—farewell ! "

FANNY L. ILES.

Who, If not God?

Who put the Pleiades in place,
Set all the satellites in motion,
Fashioned our fruitful earth in space,
Outpoured the waters of the ocean—
Who, if not God?

Who holds Orion in His hand,
Outlined with stars so bright, so clear—
Who speaks, and aye, at his command,
We reap each new revolving year—
Who, if not God?

Who regulates our day and night,
And gives us harvests plentiful,
Says that the Sun shall give us light,
The Moon shall contribute its pull—
Who, if not God?

Who man and woman didst create,
And bade to occupy the world—
Who beasts and birds decreed to mate—
Who shaped this shell so finely whorled—
Who, if not God?

The long-lived lion in its lair,
The mere ephemera, the gnat,
Each lives its limit through His care:
Whose care? Can any question that—
Whose, if not God's?

Who gives us minds so keen to know
How everything by Him is planned,
And bids us live by faith, although
Just yet, we scarce can understand—
                          Most surely God.
                          Most surely God.

                              W. ST. IVEN.

" Mine be a Home in Old England "

Mine be a home in old England,
　　Dear native isle, my queen of the sea,
Here the memories of childhood doth crowd,
　　This is the home for you, for me.

Where all glories of pleasure will greet,
　　Whether in town or proud country you be,
Every smile of its sunshine so sweet,
　　To kiss her rare blooms for summer again.

Blest country of prosperity—
　　Where liberty and freedom is known,
Here many a friendly home I know
　　In our places where I'd often roam.

In the pleasant valley by the river or sparkling brook,
　　Or on the hill by the farm field and meadow green,
How often have I loitered happily—
　　Where all my youth hath played on such a scene.

Here with equal Laws abound—
　　We toil and work for our dear land that be,
To serve our sovereign justly—
　　To live and die for thee.

JOHN O. JOSE.

The Birds' Compassion

From cot and hedge, from mansion and from tree,
We wild birds watch
These wingless creatures strange, Humanity.
With oddly-fashioned tools, they work the soil
Unceasingly, their food to gain ;
In cities, countless thousands sweat and toil.
Yet strange it is, the hardest toilers of this host
Get but a fraction of their labours' worth,
And others, toiling least, receive the most.
Their voices, then, are rarely raised in song,
But in discord and quarrelling ;
For Life for few is right ; for almost all it 's wrong.

How different we, who live unfettered, free !
The soil, by Nature tilled, us food yields all around—
'Tis there for us to seek; and one class all are we.
And then, by Nature's gift, have we the power
(A power for which Man vainly strives),
Just as the spirit wills, to fly. A life within each hour !
How else, then, but in song, our voices could we raise,
With such a life as this ?
And how, indeed, to Man could we do praise ?
And would he our monarch be,
'King of all the birds and beasts ' ?
O vain, presumptuous Man, we pity thee !

C. JAMES.

Longing for Sincerity of Heart

I often say my prayers,
But do I ever pray?
Do the wishes of my heart
Go with the words I say?
I may as well kneel down
Before a god of stone,
As offer to the living God
A prayer of words alone.
For the Lord will never hear,
Nor to those lips attend,
Whose words are not sincere.

ELIZABETH JONES.

The Value of a Smile

A girl to China wished to go,
To be kind and good to all:
Though she could not speak their tongue,
She would smile on old and young,
And try to teach them to be wise,
Then say a word for Jesus Christ.
We are always glad to see a smile,
It soothes and comforts us awhile;
It speaks of kindness in the heart,
And makes us feel we cannot part.
Like sunshine on a cloudy day,
It chases all our griefs away.

When little children are at play,
And kindly smile in all they say,
It comforts each and all around
To listen to their mirthful sound :
So we must always try to smile
On one another all the while.

ELIZABETH JONES.

Proclaiming the Word of God

The pulpit stands on sacred ground,
With space to worship all around ;
It highly polished is, and carved
With skill and graceful work of art.
Its portals only may admit
The one for holy work who's fit ;
And from within its circuit small
All plainly hear the gospel call.
The priest, arrayed in robes of white,
Oft enters it with great delight,
To preach, and teach his flock to pray,
And e'er to tread the narrow way ;
And to proclaim, with voice that rings,
The awful warning against sin.
All praise and blessing on the pulpit
And, too, on those who preach within it !
Oh, may the Gospel's joyful sound
Be heard, to bless the world around !

ELIZABETH JONES.

A Day

The cool fresh dews are on my feet,
    And in my soul
Sweet limpid dews are sparkling :
With expectation in its tread,
My spirit trips to meet the dawn :
The world is full of promise,
    And the day's begun.

High noon is on the city streets ;
    The world of men
Troop past in throngs with urgent tread :
My song remains ; my heart rides high,
And is untouched by fret or care :
I thus go through the crowded place,
    Rejoicing.

The sunset shadows are about my feet ;
    And in my heart
A kind of wistfulness of parting.
Those day-long-radiant thoughts
Are proud, high guests, and splendid-souled,
And I would have them stay :
I linger fondly with them
    As the evening falls.

O Life how glad ! How full of song !
When the dawn breaks
Clear and bright upon New Zealand hills,
How full of exultation !

How full of quiet thankfulness
    When evening falls,
And strews her pink-rose petals down the western
    clouds !
Roses of my day, roses of my day,
    How fair you've been !

                                    E. G. Jansen.

To our Grecian Princess

Welcome, welcome,
Sweet lily from over the sea,
    Marina ! Marina !
Glad welcome, dear welcome to thee.

Welcome, welcome,
With the greeting of the fleet,
And the cheering of the street,
    Marina ! Marina !
Our beautiful Grecian flower most rare,
    With lingering bloom,
    So royal, fragrant, youthful and sweet.

Welcome, welcome,
As one of our country's own,
    Marina ! Marina !
To add another bloom in our royal garden fair,
    Another bloom to grace our island home.

Welcome, welcome,
As the bride of our beloved Prince, the Empire's
  son,
    Marina ! Marina !
We hasten to meet you,
Fair Grecian, to greet you,
    With all of us Grecians and English in one.
              JOHN O. JOSE.

Music

In beautiful strains,
Your glorious echoes mingling,
Harmonic melodies, so sweet and low,
You charm the saddest heart into a song,
Still bringing love and joy where'er you go.
JOHN O. JOSE.

Autumn

Days are slowly falling in !
Now that season doth begin,
That strips the leaves from off the trees
And from the garden, with its breeze,
Which brings them whirling in the air—
We find them scattered everywhere.
JOHN O. JOSE.

Bells

Ring out, Wild Bells,
    With all your merry peals that be,
To welcome morning's gladness
    Now stealing o'er the land and sea.

In cheery tones of sweetness, sound,
    And echoes softly ringing,
Amid the Sunday sunshine
    Your message gladly bringing.
JOHN O. JOSE.

Winter

This season's full of joy and cheer,
Now the frost and snow are here;
The latter, with its winding sheet,
Which everywhere the eye doth meet,
Comes gracing Christmas, that's in sight,
In welcome gladness of delight.

Across these skies so cold and grey,
The wintry spell has dawned to stay;
Every little bird, in tamer mood,
Now, anxious, looks to us for food;
And we, at eve, round log-fire burning
   briskly, gay,
Complete the glory of a perfect Winter's day.

JOHN O. JOSE.

Spring's Awakening

Hark! to the Nightingale,
   Singing in the trees,
Sweetly chanting out her songs
   In the midnight breeze!

Now here comes the Lark,
   So merry and blithe is he,
With his song so shrill,
   Singing as loud as loud can be.

H

And, too, with the morning sun,
   Coyly peeps out Jenny Wren,
Singing, with the Robin sweet,
   Through the bonny glen.

Then follows the Cuckoo,
   Now that merry April's here,
That tells us that the Spring has come,
   So full of sweetness and of cheer.
                        JOHN O. JOSE.

My Sweet Little Rosebud

She came along, whose face was as the morning,
   And told of all the beautiful and true;
Her hair so light, with many a curl enshrining
   That dear, sweet, smiling face, with eyes grey-blue.

Her loveliness I ever shall remember,
   When first I met her, that fair golden morn;
Queenly as roses in their Summer glory,
   When kissed to fragrance by the dew at dawn.
                        JOHN O. JOSE.

To an Antique Bowl

Beneath thy polished surface, I can see
The lives of vanished nations pictured in ;
Quaint lines and strange-shaped visages of old,
Are drawn with studious care upon your shaded side ;
And visions of a craft which skilled men knew,
Is printed on the base, wherein the antique stood.
Mayhap, it stood, once on a time,
Within some ivory-pillar'd hall,
Where bards and poets hurried past,
And artists yawned and dropped their brushes ;
Or witches came, and held their strange unholy ritual,
For the attic-ghost is known to move about you.
Remote your maker, or the one who painted you !
Strange visions come upon me, as I gaze at you.
Where have you travelled, what the sights you've seen,
E'er Fate had dropt you, on the antique dealer's counter,
How many ancient battles passed by within your time ?
What strange and unbelievable tale, is writ beneath your
    lid ?
How many owners have caressed your limpid bowl,
And polished with a velvet pad, your colours, brightly
    strong ?
Perhaps sometime you've stood beside an Eastern
    throne,
And held the flowers of some dusky Queen ?
Who knows what miracles you've seen,
Before you came my way, priced at ten shillings ?

KATHLEEN C. KAY.

Sunset

When you sit in the silence and look at the sky
  All aglow with the sun's last rays,
Have you noticed, my love, how your memories fly
  To the scenes of some bygone days?

When you follow the rose-tinted, golden veil,
  Changing softly to violet and blue,
How it brings to your soul, like a sweet fairy-tale,
  All the dreams of the past anew?

And you watch in the silence, beholding the light
  Fading slowly, and yet too soon . . .
And you dream you are drifting away in the night,
  To the land of the rising moon . . .

Some sweet sunset, my love, when the shadows go by,
  All our dreams shall at last come true;
We shall drift through that rose-tinted, golden sky,
  And behold a more glorious view.

COUNT BJARNE KIRCHHOFF.

A Knight of God

If I wore the Armour of Faith,
  No mortal thing could hurt ;
If the steel were bright with Truth,
  There would be no stains or dirt.

If my sword were the Strength of God,
  All the evil I could slay ;
If my lance were the Arm of God,
  I could cast all sin away.

If my shield were God Himself,
  My Protector—I, in his care ;
And my visor His Guiding Light,
  To shine through Life and Prayer.

If my spurs were the Hands of God,
  Through Life to help me on ;
And my helmet good Deeds and Thoughts—
  All error would be gone.

If my horse never shied or turned,
  But walked the Roadway straight :—
With no burden of sin on my back,
  I'd soon reach Heaven's Gate !
                    DORIL MacMUNN KISLINGBURY.

The Cheerful "If"

If you can smile when everyone is morbid,
And be a ray of sunshine to your friends;
If you can cheer a pal who is down-hearted,
By helping him to bear the grief God sends;

If you, when things depress you, can forget them,
Think, worries cease to worry, lost to view;
If you can just remember the old saying,
To wait until the "trouble troubles you";

If when, at times, Dame Fortune seems to shun you,
While others are endowed with wealth galore,
You still can give a little help when needed,
To those who sometimes want a little more;

If though you're ever beaten by opponent,
In games at which you hoped so much for fame,
You still can take his hand and say "Good fellow!"
And tell your friends how well he "played the game";

If you are always looking on the bright side,
And making others cheerful with your smile:
Then, when you come to die you will be happy
To know your life on earth has been worth while.

                                        HADDIE KELLY.

The Emigrant's Farewell

Dear land of my Fathers, I'm leaving to-day,
And I'm sad as I bid you good-bye ;
But America calls me, so I must obey,
Tho' the thought brings a tear to my eye !
Sure, I know there's a welcome for me o'er the sea,
And they tell me 'tis all for the best ;
But where'er I may wander, my heart it will be
In my sweet Irish home in the West.

'Twas my boyhood's young dream to go over the sea,
As I'd tired of my work on the farm ;
But, then, little I knew what the parting would be
From my cottage so cosy and warm !
Oh, 'tis breaking my heart, but my tears I'll restrain,
And I'll try to turn sorrow to mirth ;
And perhaps if God wills it, I'll come back again
To the lovely old land of my birth.

HADDIE KELLY.

Contentment

Life is mostly what we make it,
Happiness is found by some ;
Others, striving, lose their balance
Looking for the joys to come.

There are thorns amidst the roses,
Pleasures, too, are marred by grief :
We should turn our back on sorrow,
For our time on earth is brief.

There are some who see the bright side,
And of hardship make the best ;
Happy he whose expectations
Are not higher than the rest.

So to those who are contented,
Let us offer up a toast :
May their span of life be lengthened,
And their pleasures be the most !

HADDIE KELLY.

Homely Philosophy

Father and Mother, Sister and Brother,
Should live in harmony with one another.
Father bears the stress of work, sometimes with sacrifice ;
Mother bears all this and more, ofttimes at any price :
Children with them life's burdens should share
Living would then be freed from much care—
Free of regrets, for things left undone ;
Free of regrets, for many things done ;
Free on life's pathway, ever to roam,
Thinking of good things once done at our home.

FRANK LAFSER, Jr.

What is Love ?

What is Love? it who can explain?
It comes like a dream, and may leave just the same.
Love is a mist that comes in the night—
By morning you'll find Love is holding you tight :
Love is a laugh for all those who don't care,
But for me disappointment I found hard to bear :
Love has its thrills, its laughs, and its tears,
And Lovers are parted for many long years :
But, still, what is Love? it who can explain?
It's just an affection we all hope to gain.

FRANK LAFSER, Jr.

The Old Klondyke Trail

There's a trail that runs thru' my old homestead,
A trail that has known the living and dead;
It runs as straight as the flight of a crow,
Over the high lands and over the low.

And it's known the tread of the patient ox,
With its Red River cart—two wheels and a box;
It's felt the tramp of a million crazed men—
Some lived to return down that trail—and then—

Many found graves by that hurrying trail,
And with bleached ox-ribs that formed a rail
To mark the spot where a wanderer fell—
His greed for gold was his ticket to hell.

Blasting and tearing the breast of the earth,
Raping the land with a devil's mirth,
They bartered their souls in exchange for gold—
Honour and God and friend were sold.

And those were the days back in '49,
When the life of man wasn't worth a dime;
The law of the gun, the law of the pack—
The strong went forward, but the weak went back.

But the earth is old, and woefully wise,
Guarding her wealth with a million lies:
If only the trail had the lips to tell
Of the men who passed on their way to hell!

Forgotten now those restless souls who hiked
Along this trail, the magnet, gold—Klondyke!
The sharp-cut trail's now soft with passing years,
Grown thick with grass as Spring again appears.

V. H. LYNE, D.C.M., M.M.

Farm Lyrics

I'm Mary Jane, and very plain,
And always do my work ;
But there *are* jobs I'd like to shirk.

At 6 a.m. I start agen
My usual daily round ;
No better maid is found.

" Hullo," says I, as creeping by
The Master's bedroom door,
" 'Tis long past half-past four ! "

The kettle's on, I sing a song—
A cup of tea
For you and me.

My Master, Farmer Giles,
So full of smiles,
Comes down to see his cup of tea.

A kindly man, he has a plan,
As you will see. He likes plain me.
He's got a chicken-farm,
And can tell a mighty yarn.

I like this one. When work is done,
He'll take a run
In his Rolls-Royce.
His gentle voice

Bids me make my home
Where he does roam—
Upon his chicken-farm,
Where there's no harm.

So Mary Jane did change her name
To Mrs. Farmer Giles;
    and both
Did travel miles and miles.

JOAN LEIGHTON.

Rondeau

THE DÉBUTANTE

Launched on the World! Your simple dress
Becomes you well. I must confess
You captivate my willing eye:
No other maiden far or nigh
Can rival you in comeliness.

    Quick changes on your face express
    The thoughts your eyes already guess,
    Like sunbeams from a summer sky
    Launched on the World.

I've watched you grow in beauty—yes,
I love to see your huge success,
Sweet seventeen! Alas, that I
Am twice as old! Forgive the sigh—
From an old bachelor in distress—
    Launched on the World.

F. G. LEVIEN.

Heaven's Harvest Home

Thank God for the rain,
The shadows and pain,
Which both come alike to us all ;
The hot sunshine hardens
The fields and the gardens,
And they welcome the raindrops small.

It is so in life :
The worries and strife,
The comforts and blessings, that come,
Are all sent in love
By our Father above,
To fit us for " Heaven's Harvest Home."

Then rise from the dust,
In Christ put thy trust,
Nor slacken thine own small endeavour.
Do bravely thy part,
Hope on and take heart,
While trusting in thy God for ever.

Oh, what blissful joy,
Which never will cloy,
When we meet on that golden floor ;
With Christ walk in white,
Where there is no night,
And parting and death are no more !

The angels will stand
On that heavenly strand,
Rejoicing that we are forgiven ;
We'll all see Christ's face,
And the throne of His Grace,
At the " Harvest Home of Heaven."

Hallelujah !
GEORGIANNA THIRZA CHILD.
(Blind).

The Downs

I love those friendly, wandering Downs
That shelter many Sussex towns
From wind and rain and howling gale :
Those whitened scars do tell a tale
Of many fights 'gainst fearful odds,
With weapons fashioned by the gods.

When vision was but fun and clowns,
I went to school beneath the Downs :
I climbed up rugged paths of chalk,
Upon their rolling backs to walk :
I cried when broiling Summer came
With drought and fires, my friends to maim.

And now, beneath their friendly slopes,
The Downs do shelter all my hopes :
I never fear on stormy nights
When gods and Downs do have their fights ;
They'll keep her warm and safe and well,
Even against the arms of hell.

I. M. F. LIGHTLY

Rondeau

MY HEART'S DELIGHT

My heart's delight, why dost thou seem
So near to me when'er I scheme
To make the long, long days go by
Here by the Lakes of Italy,
Thou my sole thought, my only theme !

  Bright are thine eyes ; brighter, I deem,
  Than the blue wavelets' spangled gleam
  Rising and falling tenderly,
  My heart's delight !

Flow with my thoughts, flow on swift stream,
Down to the shore where seagulls scream.
Perchance one night a bird may fly,
Telling my love for her I sigh
'Neath scorching sun or pale moonbeam—
  My heart's delight !

F. G. LEVIEN.

Camouflage

Oh ! April is the time to woo,
  When magic fills the sky,
And maidens, willing all the while,
  Pretend that they are shy ;

And when the fairy of your dreams
  Eludes your longing hold,
And will not give the chance to tell
  The tale that would be told,

But, running, leaves you to pursue
  Wherever she may lead,
The while Apollo in the wood
  Pipes love-songs on his reed.

How sweet to catch the nimble miss,
  After a laughing race,
And see the beacon-fires of love
  Aglow upon her face ;

And hear her warm, red lips confess
  The truth divined for long,
Apollo, piping in the shade
  The same old lilting song.

Oh ! April is the time to woo,
  When magic fills the sky,
And maidens, willing all the while,
  Pretend that they are shy.
Ĺric MacLaren.

This is the Day

This is the day—not yesterday or to-morrow—
This day is ours to live, to love, to do !
This is the day to make our new beginnings,
With high resolves, while all the world is new.

This is the day—not yesterday or to-morrow—
To-day's the day in which to do our part
To usher in the age which brave men dreamed of,
The age for which they laboured long for naught.

This is the day—not yesterday or to-morrow—
To build upon foundations fearless souls have laid ;
This is the day to right the wrongs of ages ;
This is the day for action long delayed.

This is the day ! Let us be up and doing—
To-day, with all its golden dawn, is here ;
To-day let's live and make our lives worth living
To greet that golden age we see more clear.

ETHEL E. MEREDITH.

Trains

When I was young I wished to be
  An engine driver bold,
That I might drive the great express
  That down the main line rolled.

At three o'clock each afternoon,
  Upon the bridge I stood,
To watch it roaring under me
  As all expresses should.

But when I grew a bigger boy,
  I had another plan—
I wished to be a surly guard,
  And travel in the van;

For then I'd have a whistle shrill,
  And flags both green and red,
And, best of all, I'd board the train
  While moving on ahead.

But now that I have gone to school
  I may not speak of trains,
For if I mentioned engines
  They would kick me for my pains.

But still I love the railroad bright,
  The shining metal line,
The signals, trucks and carriages,
  And wish that they were mine.

P. F. MACHIN.

To the Unforgiving

Someday, perhaps, there'll be no smile for you,
  Perhaps for me no hand within mine own ;
And none will seem, somehow, to us so true ;
  And one will wake some morn to life alone !

Someday there'll be for one of us ' the break ',
  And would one be a little sad, or find
Some smile to answer new, perhaps to make
  The world a fairer place—and life more kind ?

Someday, however far the one may walk,
  There'll be no meeting ! one of us will say,
They miss the old familiar word of greeting
  That shortened so our longest, roughest way.

Someday for one, beneath a cold, calm brow
  May two eyes close on a *forgiving* smile,
One will be left to pray, " For pity now,
  Dear God, make life's long way ' a little while ' ! "
                              FRANCIS MANSELL-RHYS.

Great Pilot Death

Great Pilot, Death, why do men fear thee so?
  So dread the tolling of the warning bell?
Heed not thy voice that through the last long watch,
  Sounds o'er the rising wave, the call, " All's well ! "

Is it that unlike grief, thou coming once,
  Few know thy face? then, walking by the side,
How blessed are they, who, knowing, wait thy touch
  To close down lids o'er eyes set Heaven-wide.

'Tis strange that men should call thee end of life,
  And talk of eventide when it is morn;
Should fear to draw the sable veil aside,
  To greet the harbour lights of breaking dawn !

I know that some who rend that dreaded veil,
  Who speak of thee, with tears, as life's sad end,
Will, glimpsing through the misty, veil-torn space,
  Find in thy features—face to face—a friend—

A friend whose cold, grey fingers point the way
  To some calm place of waiting after strife,
Where we at last shall see the words revealed,
  " I am the Resurrection, *and* the Life ! "

FRANCIS MANSELL-RHYS.

To My Black Cat

Minet,
If I could only understand your feline soul,
Hidden midst external charms,
How happy should I be.
But Sphinx-like, in your black array,
Elusive, complex entity.

You prowl, you stray;
Entering in at break of day,
Wet with the dew of morn, you come to couch,
And dream of conquests yet undone.

No wonder Egypt's dynasties worshipped you,
Creature of mystery.

JOHN MARSHALL.

To Nature

Nature enfold me, let me forget
Life's tragic sorrows, and all that doth fret;
Nature uplift me, bathe me in Light,
Beauty unsullied, be my delight.
Nature triumphant, mirror Divine,
All ages claim thee, sweet anodyne.

JOHN MARSHALL.

Snobs

Pompous is their name,
And pompous they remain,
Viewing the World from an altitude,
Commiserating the multitude.

" Thank God," they say,
" I'm not of man's clay ! "
Forgetting The Son who became one.

JOHN MARSHALL.

Trees in Autumn

Trees, thy branches bare,
Leaves wrought with sweeping winds from Zephyr's
    blast,
Withered, scattered, shrouded in Earth's clasp.
Yet e'en those boughs, now destitute of lovely green,
Will yet revive in Spring-time's splendrous sheen.

JOHN MARSHALL.

A Plea for Youth

*(On hearing men who should know better, discuss the
" Next War ")*

They are so young !
We dare not think that death should call them yet ;
Not for a little while,
Till they have known
A resting from youth's adolescent fret.

They are but boys—
Like growing trees in Springtime when the sun
Breathes into them his warmth—
And they perceive,
In silence, of a freedom still to come,

When they shall reap
The fruit that work of youth shall yield to them,
And, looking back,
Recall youth's restless days,
And be content to leave the past a dream.

Leave them in peace !
All we may ask is work of hand and brain
To serve a nation's cause,
The empty pride
Of battle won gives them not life again !

LUCY MAUND.

Life

Sunlight strewn across our path,
  The scented smell of musk ;
Sunlight dancing everywhere,
  Then—dusk.

Dusk, the setting of the sun,
  The world in rose-hued light,
Shadows deep'ning, moonbeams dim,
  Then—night.

SYLVIA MCGARVIE.

Enchantment

The moonbeams peeping,
  The stars above,
The whole world sleeping,
  The night and love.
Your arms around me,
  The love of youth ;
Your dear, seeking lips,
  My hungry mouth !

SYLVIA MCGARVIE.

Christmas Greetings

I hope that this Message you will not now spurn,
Because I, myself, its Lesson did learn—
The Message of Jesus Who died on the Cross.
It all is pure thought, and every soul's rhyme,
And comes through the merit of Christ-love, divine.

It happiness means, wealth, health that's untold,
To those who to it heart and mind will unfold;
So please do not cast on one side, with a toss,
This message of Truth, of the Man on the Cross.

His true wish is this, for each soul that's new-born,
That he should on this, and on each Christmas Morn,
Hold Christ-love—the magnetic power of pure thought.
Electric it is, and e'er brings instant healing,
For the soul filled with it is with God's Spirit fraught.

By the Spirit of Truth God's battle is won—
This Spirit is one with the Father and Son;
And the Son Himself says, " I'm the Bright Morning
    Star ! "
So come all, and worship Him, come from afar.   Amen !

MARY S. McINNIS.

The Cure

If you'll not worry,
But stop mental strain,
I know you'll never,
Have any more pain.
For, if the truth
You'll try to find,
Our troubles commence
And end in our mind.
Therefore, when with love
You o'ercome all fear,
Both sickness and sin
Will all be gone, Dear.
So no matter what
Our creed may be,
We must have faith,
Both you and me;
And when through Truth
The right way we begin,
We know life's eternal,
No matter the end.

MARY S. McINNIS.

The Prairie Sunset

Beneath the clouds the sunset spreads,
Its colours bright and bold,
Making the fields and prairie look
Like a fiery sheet of gold.
Breezes blow! As the sun sinks low,
Gathering waves of heat,
Pouring the fresh and crispy air,
Into evening cool—" We meet."

The Prairie Sunset is a scene
That lingers far and wide :
We sit on hill-sides, close to lanes,
And watch the flickering shadows hide.
Cattle and great flocks of sheep
Graze in twilight's loom,
Filling up on the grassy plains,
To rest by the silvery moon.

MRS. THOMAS J. MOHN.

Kindness

Kindness is a vivid act
  That crowns the world with pleasure;
A weary thought, a tempted mind,
  Will find in it a treasure.

Many a storm has anchored safe
  When kindness stooped to enter,
Beckoning, with its binding threads
  To mend a spurnful temper.

Swiftly do the moments pass
  When kind deeds flutter gaily;
A peaceful home we're sure to find,
  Where kindness hovers daily.

Remember, as we hustle by,
  To greet with kind words true;
If sadness comes and nestles down,
  Kindness will drift to you.

MRS. THOMAS J. MOHN.

My Love is at the Helm

I know no fear : if the wild winds blow,
Or the billows loudly roar,
My heart with joy doth overflow,
To see my love once more.
The tide may ebb, and the tide may flow,
The tide may ebb, and the tide may flow :
I know no fear, if the wild winds blow,
My Love is at the Helm,
My Love is at the Helm.

I know no fear, if my love is near,
His heart I still hold dear ;
And the smile upon his loving face
Makes Heaven appear more near,
The tide may ebb, and the tide may flow,
The tide may ebb, and the tide may flow :
I know no fear, if my love is near,
My Love is at the Helm,
My Love is at the Helm.

I know no fear ! For the storms of life
But drift our vessel on,
Through the waters of strife, to the Heavenly life
We all must enter on.
The tide may ebb, and the tide may flow,
The tide may ebb, and the tide may flow :
I know no fear, if Christ be near,
For He will guide the Helm,
For He will guide the Helm.

E. M. MOODY.

My Brogue-Shoes

Oh, you shall come, my brogues, to-day,
A trip with me down Devon way ;   :
I could not think of walking there
Without you two, my bonny pair :
This hiking would not be complete,
Had I not you to guard my feet.

Just you and I alone will tour
Through pretty lanes, o'er open moor ;
Along the roads down to the sea,
You'll love to tramp along with me :
We'll slur through shingle and through sand—
I'm sure I heard you say, " That's grand."

We'll crunch through woods, and grip high hills,
Climb farm gates, pass by water-mills,
While farmer nods, and says with grin,
" Thems the fine shoes for hiking in ! "
And when I tell the pals to me
You've been, I'm sure he will agree.

But he won't know that, walking on,
I put you down with rhyming song ;
That raising you, I add a bit,
Or check, to see that all doth fit :
This present song's all due to you,
So much you please, my small brogue-shoe.

Oh, when you're worn (sometime, no doubt),
It will be sad to cast you out,
For you have given service splendid,
And I shall grieve when it is ended:
Still, I suppose, 'twill have to be.
The parting of my brogues and me.

FLORENCE MOUNTAIN.

Courage

Be not out at the count of ten,
  Stand up to the foe and fight;
Be honourable, brave British men;
  In danger take courage, not flight.

Think of all those who gave their lives
  In the terrible days of yore;
Who left their homes, parents and wives,
  To help in England's war!

Their gallant deeds we'll ne'er erase;
  Of cowards there were none;
They, when death stared them in the face,
  Heroically fought on.

With such example for your guide,
  Speak from your hearts, and say,
" With God for ever at my side,
  I'll fight for ever and aye."

PAULINE W. NAUGHTON.

Earthbound

Help the eyes of the blind here and now to be opened ;
　The earth-bound and selfish, oh, God, may they see
Thy love and Thy beauty around and above them !
　Awaken and guide them to light and to Thee.

That they may behold Thee with wonder and gladness,
　And ears all attuned to Thy music around,
Show them how rich a store may be had for the asking
　And in giving, not taking, true joy may be found.

ETHEL E. MEREDITH.

On the Sea-beach

On a moonlit night, when the bright Moon
On the myriad waves doth quiver,
I think and dream of thee, my Dear!
When the silvery rays of the orb of heaven
Bathe the sea in rapture.
And waves dance in ecstasy and endeavour
To reach the Moon in high heaven,
Thy dark-blue eyes encourage me
To march on in life's struggle,
To fight the ills and face the battle,
To court the bullet, if need be.
'Tis joy to die in dreams of thee
When spreads the Moon her rays on me,
And the Cares of Earth take holiday:
It is not death, but passing away
Into the dreamland of the Moon,
Where only thy true love holds sway.

D. Mukherji.

Mira Bāi

(Mahārāni Mira was a devotee of Lord Krishna, and left her hearth and home in quest of God, in the full bloom of her youth. She renounced the world, left her happy home and loving husband, on a Holy Pilgrimage, at the comparatively early age of twenty-eight.)

Can the loving embrace of the Mahārāna hold her back ?
Stay her who's heard Thy Call and chosen her track ?
She runs mad after Thee, singing loud songs of joy ;
Throws away life's pleasures, like a discarded toy.
She tramples, under her foot, all worldly tie,
Rejects luxury as an obnoxious lie ;
Bonds of love die away like drops of dew
When the sacred Fire of Divine Love is enkindled
      in golden hue.
King's angry gestures can no longer her control,
She who has seen the Vision and chosen her goal ;
Where love has failed, Power can never win—
Power abused is but another name for sin ;
She who has set her heart on dreams of Thee,
Flies from King's embrace, and runs in divine glee.
Hark ! hold back ! do not hold her in your arms,
No longer can she give you her Heavenly charms !

Vain-glorious Rānā, blinded with power,
You have dashed to pieces her Love's bower,
To smithereens broken her stately temple,
Her higher Love but with fire to enkindle.
You have stopped her in divine meditation,
Turned the serene sea of Love into high Commotion.

The sting shall eat into your very heart,
Take you out from the Palace to the desert,
Make you feel lonely and sad.
Sadder still—in grief, half mad—
You will think of Mira, dear,
Who will no longer your wailings hear.
The Lord of Mewar shall follow her footsteps,
And run there to call her back, in grace,
Only to find her lifeless form,
Richer in beauty and in Form !

D. MUKHERJI.

Kathran

Come—
       don't be afeard.
A velvety green sward is keeping—
      A blue canopy above;
Only the stars are peeping—
What do they know about love ?
  Me ?
      I'm not skeered !

SAM RANDALL.

The Sea-Gull

Just one lonely sea-gull,
  With heart so true and brave;
Oh, he has seen many a gale,
  And breasted many a wave.

Through the water gliding,
  His webbed feet paddles make,
How gracefully he goes slipping
  Across the shining lake!

He now climbs out on to the shore,
  A beautiful lonely gull,
And gazes 'round towards the boat,
  To me within its hull.

Then to the wing he swiftly takes,
  And glides so gracefully away,
Unto the far side of the lake,
  To wait the closing of the day.

How beautiful God's creatures come,
  How swiftly they do go,
To teach us how, beneath the sun,
  He loves us all just so!

NITA MYERS.

My Garden of Dreams

Oh, where have the blossoms of Summer all flown,
Their tints like the morning sun's glow?
And where are the colours that Autumn has thrown?—
They bloom in a garden I know:
A garden where Winter ne'er enters at all,
But roses for ever entwine
Around the old sundial near to the wall,
In that dear Dream-garden of mine.

Forget-me-nots, they are a-blossoming, too,
Beneath an old apple-tree's shade;
And hyacinths, yellow and red, white and blue,
Make pleasant a shadowy glade.
Twines sweet honeysuckle to make me a bower,
Wherein to dream long hours away;
A pink hawthorn tree is for ever in flower—
In Winter as well as in May.

The pansy is lifting its shy little head
From out of its wide-spreading leaves;
The poppies are blooming, tho' Autumn has fled,
And clematis climbs round the eaves.
The jasmine, so starlike, is flowering, too,
And everywhere sweet peas entwine,
Reflecting the sunshine in daintiest hues,
And cheering that garden of mine.

Whatever the season, whatever the clime,
The sun sheds his glorious beams
On rosemary, larkspur, and sweet-scented thyme,
That bloom in my Garden of Dreams,

So if you are lonely, and things have gone wrong,
And sorrows round your heart entwine,
I'll take you in hand and will teach you a song
In that ever green garden of mine.

MARY NICHOLSON.

The Tryst

Where grows the whisp'ring waving sedge,
Close beside the streamlet's edge,
Beneath a willow's graceful bend,
Where woods begin and meadows end,
    I wait.

A crimson sunset fills the west;
The lark still soars above his nest
As his sweet evensong he trills;
And now each nerve within me thrills—
    She comes.

Her happy laugh and lilting lay
Scatter soft joys around her way,
And stay the approaching shades of night :
The sun has gone—yet all is light,
    She's here.

HENRY NORMAN.

The Land of Promise

Light as spindrift my spirits soar;
Lovelier Nature's beauty glows;
The sun's rays warm as ne'er before;
All things to me are coloured rose
Now 'tis my rapture to surprise
The love-light, dear one, to your eyes.

The song-bird's soulful ecstasy
Before a rival's claims must bow;
Though thrilling still their melody,
A sweeter charms my ear, for now
New music makes my heart rejoice,—
The love-note, dear one, in your voice.

A vision haunts my waking dreams,—
The Land of Promise, gleaming bright;
A beauteous land of murmuring streams
Bedecked with flowers for our delight:
There Love will keep our hearts in tune
To win a lifelong honeymoon.

ERNEST NELSON.

The Reapers

The Summer sun is glowing on the fields so bright and
  gay,
The fields that, ripe to harvest, now show gold beneath
  its ray ;
And in the distance, far away, is heard the reapers'
  voice—
To gather all, in safety, in will make their hearts rejoice.

They love the time of harvest, though 'tis e'er a time of
  work,
A time when all must labour—there's no room for those
  who shirk.
We see the old farm waggon there, up-piled with golden
  grain,
Made ripe both by the Summer sun and heavy showers
  of rain.

The children, they are happy, there, behind the reapers'
  course,
And all triumphant when they get their promised ride
  a-horse ;
The rabbits, they view, with dismay, the rows cut, one
  by one—
Where will they ride, they wonder, when the last one
  shall be done.

Their enemies, the dogs, are there as well, alert for
  prey—
They spot poor Bunny by his tail, and chase him far
  away :

Their fell pursuers some escape, but some are killed
    and torn—
No more they'll see their burrows or feast on the farmer's
    corn.

The farmer's horse is all attent unto its master's will—
Now o'er the field it paces slow, or patient waits, and
    still.
The farmer, he for sunset waits, his eyes then scan the
    sky—
He knows, if golden is the West, the morrow will be
    dry.

The fields will soon deserted be, the sun is sinking low ;
'Tis eventide, and o'er the hills the gentle breezes blow ;
The harvest moon is rising o'er the earth so richly blest ;
Now man and horse their labour leave, to take their
    well-earned rest.
                                 EILEEN G. NETHERCOTT.

The Gate

A dark and misty morn
Heralds the hour of fate,
And in the glimm'ring dawn
Looms over all—the Gate.

Into the hostile fire,
The road is rough and strait,
Over torn earth and wire,
And then beyond—the Gate?

And now the moment's near
That spares nor small nor great,
For each, in hope or fear,
Waits, near or far—the Gate.

Why should I dread the lot
That must come soon or late?
Oh, God of Battles, shame me not,
Should I pass through the Gate!

HENRY NORMAN.

To a Flower

Little bud of mirth and madness,
May this be a happy day,
All your world be filled with gladness
And no shadow pass your way.
When the bud bursts forth in blossom
In the early days of Spring,
Full of hopes and expectations,
Gilded flower, exotic thing.
When the Autumn winds are sighing
And the leaves begin to fall,
All in Nature slowly dying,
Youth and hope beyond recall.
Time on silver wings is fleeting,
Shrouded in a veil of years,
And the journey's end is weeping,
Disillusionment and tears.

Mrs. O'Dogherty.

The Chart

I came upon a chart one day :
  It was a plan of life's highway—
Of the broad and of the narrow way,
  The works on each, and how they pay.

The road so broad, so blithe and gay,
  The giddy multitude did throng ;
Those travelling on the narrow way
  Firmly repulsed the things all wrong.

As I gazed on the separate scenes,
  The plain-marked contrast I defined :
Each in a different kind of way
  Appeased the needs of heart and mind.

Along the Broad way, as they walked,
  Almost before they were aware,
In dazzling show, or some excitement, keen,
  They found their souls with sin did share.

Their joys upon the narrow path
  Were of a different mould ;
By sacrifice and service, they
  Did work of God unfold.

This work will silently go on,
  Though by the world unseen;
For we need not one moment doubt
  The world will be redeemed.

But yet the harvest, it will come,
   That last great reaping-day,
And then, with wheat and tares apart,
   There still will be two ways.

                              ANNIE PADDY.

Memories

Just a pile of faded letters,
   Tied together and kept through the years;
Some were written mid joyous laughter,
   Some, maybe, with a heart full of tears.

Just a bundle of worn-out pictures,
   Reaching like ghosts from out of the past;
Those good old times cannot return, Dear,
   But the memories will always last.

They tell of the old, old story,
   Of the love 'tween a girl and a lad;
But these are specially dear to me,
   From my Mum to my Darlingest Dad.

                              MARGERY PALMER.

Baby's Second Birthday

Can another year have passed
　Since your little life began?
Why, how those sturdy legs can run!
　You're getting quite a grown-up man.

I can hear those little feet,
　Up and down go pitter-patter;
In your own wee baby language,
　How that little tongue does chatter

What can I wish you this year,
　For a precious gift that's rare?
You've already got an engine,
　And a great big Teddy Bear.

Always cheery words to greet you,
　As you grow and tramp life's miles,
I'll just wish this " Little Man,"
　Nothing else but Sunshine's smiles.

MARGERY PALMER.

Nemesis

As a sprightly Genie awoke one day,
And rose with the sun, he was heard to say,
" A mission have I to Mortals who fight
For the wealth of the world, with joy-killing blight.

" And He who commands me I must obey,
No hesitation—let there come what may.
I am the factor that Justice desires
To determine all that oppression requires."

So into the wide, busy world he went,
With patience his time in watching was spent.
Those who had riches and names that were great,
He said as he watched, " To prove them I'll wait."

So, in time, he saw what most did not see—
That mortals were not what they seemed to be :
Smiling, courteous, to all whom they met,
A cloak of deception to snare them was set.

Kindness and sympathy sundered by greed,
Left nothing but grief for poor souls in need ;
Unscrupulous business methods had they,
Robbing the poor ones of money each day.

At last came a time when Nemesis said,
" Your limit is reached, your fortune is sped.
Thou fallest by greed to a selfish end :
This their reward, who for riches contend."

Thus Nemesis came to mortals who fought
For riches and power that millions have sought ;
Who sacrificed Heaven for hope of gain,
And awoke to the Truth—It was all in vain !

CHAS C. PASSMORE.

Retrospect

O friend of past days, who shall say that lives are lived
    apart,
When, from the vista of long years, Communion lives,
    of heart ?
E'en tho' the mist of silence hide, tho' distance still
    divide,
Yet kindred souls by thought and prayer defy sere
    time, or tide.

O blessed mem'ry, to us giv'n, recalling what has been !
Men call it but the " husks " of time, yet treasure deep,
    I meen :
Thoughts of some dear one, tenderly, in inmost depth
    of soul,
These help despondent, weary lives to climb to higher
    goal.

Our hearts are fashioned by the Will Whose creed is,
    Love endured ;
And souls are balanced in the Hand Divine, tho' age
    immured.

L

Blind to immensity of Love?   Ah, no, One under-
    stands :
We'll leave our present, future, past, in His most
    generous Hands.

What mortal living on this earth can gauge another's
    need,
Tho' nature's instincts teach us how our own deep
    needs to heed?
Yet we can realize the Hope—His promise to mankind—
While waiting here, in friendship's love, and perfect
    faith of mind.

PAMELA PHILLIPS.

Reflections

A wingèd bird I met, while walking by the shore;
It placed me on its back, and up it 'gan to soar.
And up and up I went, and saw on earth, below,
The foaming seas to which the mountain rivers flow.

The orbèd star of light withdrew its scorching day,
And her lofty shelf, the moon began to sway.
In ecstasy I gazed through space—oh, great my joy!—
A happy child that smiled upon its dearest toy.

Beneath my feet I saw a spreading curtain, blue,
And twinkling spots of gold—alas, they were too few!
And in and out among these blazing points, a ship
A shining vessel, huge and round—did dance and skip.

Sometimes a sheet of water blotted out a light,
And then I sorrowed for the lighthouse keeper's plight.
And now and then the floating circle would be lost,
As o'er its sparkling decks a wave King Neptune tossed.

Then up at Heaven's sky I looked, and saw—the same!
There was my silver boat, the moon, that played her
    game
Of hide-and-seek amidst the stars and planets great,
That stud with jewels love's divinely azure slate.

And there were cloudy seas, through which the vessel's
    ray
Did slowly plough and push its weary, gasping way;

And thus I wondered if this firmament of ours
Were but a mirror with some wondrous, magic powers.

But then I dropped from off my flying dolphin's neck—
In time to dodge my mount's ferocious, vicious peck—
And down I dropped and fell amidst a lotus lake—
The splash resounding made the little fishes quake !

CHARLES PEGGOTTE.

The Voice of the Mighty Organ

I'm just a gipsy maid, with gipsy ways,
Who freely roams the commons, night and day.
My heart was free until I heard a haunting melody
Played on an organ by someone—a song I'll ne'er forget ;
'Twas loud and strong, 'twas sweet and low ; the words
 I do not know,
But, oh, that wondrous melody, it lingers with me yet !
 I need no camp-fires now to keep me warm,
 Nor song-birds nor guitars my mind to charm ;
Still with that melody my heart is burning,
To hear it once again my heart is yearning.
In memory I hear it still come creeping o'er the air ;
Both night and day it haunts me,
Both night and day it taunts me,
The voice of the mighty organ as it rumbles through the
 woods ;
Vibrating there, it fans the flame that burns my very
 soul.
Despite brick walls and miles between, it penetrates them
 all,
The voice of the mighty organ as it stirs each leafy hall.
It seemed to me a gentle touch that played on that
 keyboard,
But it could stir up storms at sea, or lullaby, play,
 sweet and low,
 Evoking storms of memories.
I need no glittering lights and velvet chairs in halls so
 bright,

With fern-bed in the open air, and no one near to see
    the tears,
As the voice of the mighty organ I hear rumbling over-
    head.

The song dies down, 'tis hushed and still. My heart,
    it then doth ponder on
The man whose fingers have such skill; but we ne'er
    meet, we twain.
Then softly through the trees, again there comes that
    haunting melody,
        And for a while I live once more;
But all too soon both man and song are gone,
Leaving behind an ache and pain and a heart like molten
    lead,
As the voice of the mighty organ still rumbles on o'er-
    head.

FLORRIE PHILLIPS.

Eventide

Hushed is the song of birds,
Gently the streamlet flows,
Returning are the herds,
  At eventide.

Hist'ry repeats her theme,
Nature is lulled to rest,
While stars begin to gleam
  At eventide.

Dark is the meadow green,
Gently the zephyrs play
A youth and maiden 'tween,
  At eventide.

Hushed is all sound save sighs,
Hearts beat in unison
Pledging their troth, they rise,
  At eventide.

Softly wend they their way,
Arm-in-arm down the aisle;
They're man and wife to-day,
  At eventide.

Happy—they knew no strife—
For fifty summers full;
Calmly they've reached in life
  Their eventide.

Hard by yon rill they sleep :
Hushed are their voices now ;
There where the willows weep,
'Tis eventide.

C. W. PHILLIPS

Night

Thou art not dreadful to me, sable night :
Softer thy touch than falling of the dews.
Thy hours more peaceful than those of the light
They are the hours that I would ever choose :
After the toil, the worry and the fret,
How sweet the cares of day-time to forget !

Where dost thou dwell? In Oblivion's stream,
Or in the cavernous gloom of the deep sea,
Spinning lace fantasies, cobwebby dreams,
Brewing the drug that sets all mortals free?
Silent, secluded, wise sorceress, thou,
Give me a taste of that healing draught now.

Weaver of fancies, of phantoms, of dreams,
Lady, who closest the gates of the sun,
Goddess, who fashions the silver moonbeams
And lightest the stars when the day-time is done,
Gently come stealing o'er land and o'er sea,
Bearing the incense of visions to me.

Lady, who bringest the balm of repose,
Guardian true of the dark hours of sleep,
Decked with the reddest of flowers that grow,
Shod with the twilight that purples the deep,
Bring me release from my burden of care,
Leave me the poppies that hang from thy hair.

ENID M. PICKEL.

Shadows

Shadows steal across my path,
At the setting sun,
Try to hide the loveliness
Of the day that's done.
But the clouds hold high the glow
Shining from afar—

O'er the shadow of the Cross,
Heaven's gates ajar.

ENID M. PICKEL.

If we only understood

Could we read the minds around us,
    Take one little peep within,
Know the reason for some action,
    Of a small, or some great, sin,
Should we judge our friends and neighbours
    Quite so harshly?—see no good
In a life by God created,
    If we only understood?

Could we know the cares and sorrows,
   Understand the bitter strife,
Know the struggles or temptations,
   See the reason why that life
Chose to follow down the pathway
   Where the Angels fear to tread,
Should we blame him quite so harshly?
   Should we pity, then, instead?

If we understood the motive,
   Knew the powers at work within,
Judged not by the outer roughness,
   Even though we loathed the sin .
Should we see beyond the evil,
   Glean a little grain of good
   In that life of sin and sorrow,
   If we only understood ?

Ah ! we pass our judgments harshly,
   As we walk along life's way ,
When, instead of cruel derision,
   Kindness might some evil stay.
For since God says, " Love one another,"
   Bow, then, to His Great Command;
Forgive, as we would be forgiv'n,
   And some day we'll understand.

EFFIE PIKE.

England

England, my beautiful England, I love thine everything, England,

From the princeliest peaks of thy mountains to the lowliest flower of thy meadows.

Thou art dear when the sun shines clear through an azure and gold-tinted heaven ;

Thou art dear when the mournful rain descends, cooling and fresh, to thy bosom.

I love thy fields—from above they appear as a blanket of patchwork ;

Still more do I love thy gardens, those dear, perfect miniature gardens,

The rose-gardens, fountains and statues, the velvety lawns, and the borders

Where bloom innumerable flowers, a medley of brilliant colour ;

Blue delphinium and monk's hood, and foxglove, and glorious sunflower,

Lift their lovely heads skywards, ambitious to clamber to Heaven,

While modest viola clings, content, to the breast of the mother.

And what is more charming, England, than thy country lanes, with their hedgerows—

Hedgerows of elder and rose, of blackthorn and hawthorn and laurel ?

There sings the common thrush, and the robin chirps through the winter.

I love thy forests and woods—the remains of an old
    sylvan England—

Where once wild animals prowled, and fought, and
    killed, and were hunted.

Yonder I see a shack, made lovely by snowy-white
    roses

Which scramble in wild profusion o'er the bare, black
    boards of the hovel.

England, thy people are generous; they are loving and
    simple-hearted;

Yet they would die for thee gladly, for they cherish
    thee dearly, as I do.

This moment especially I love thee, for all is drifting to
    slumber;

The soft-dripping rain tells the secret of that lusciously
    beautiful greenness

Which can only be seen in the woods, and the hedge-
    rows, and meadows, of England;

Every sound is stilled, except, far off, in the distance,

The noisy bark of a dog, and the plaintive wail of an
    infant

That is kept too long from its cradle by a thoughtless,
    or ignorant, parent.

Ay, indeed thou art beautiful, England, my homeland,
    my country;

No other country is like thee, nor has been, nor yet ever
    will be;

England can only be England, rising supreme above all
    things.

                             ADA M. PILGRIM

The Ocean

Roll on, roll on, thou deep, dark blue Ocean!
Be restless, rolling till the vast aeon!
All power of earthly man's too low to think
How in what endless waves thou e'er rollst on.
No human shape can change thy boundless shape.
The live moon seeks a joy high o'er thee, all alone;
Æolus o'er thy tripping waves still his harp tunes;
Younglings delight to dance upon the yellow dunes.

Amidst thy raving billows the fishermen float;
Across thy rutless road the huge ships float—
Thy madden'd billows upwards shoot in vain;
Pass o'er the rating raven clouds and rain.

All hail, thou father of all scattered isles!
The vast known hemispheres float firm on thee;
The broken, insphered shards of this earth's pile,
A sparkling string of priceless pearls for thee!

Hail to thee, thou wedded Lord of Rivers,
Thine impatient, countless, charming partners!
They, small and great alike, run eager race
To join their lovely lord in keen embrace.

What gorgeous treasures are hid thee within!
What priceless gems and jewels, all unseen!
Your cavern is the home of a vast mine
Where priceless pearls and corals endless shine.

The ruddy Phoebus cools his fiery torch,
That animates the earth on his curved march,
Only in thy measureless acqua shore,
And at thy next end lights again once more.

R. B. PINGLAY.

A Sonnet

Sweet, smile, and wake in me, like yon full moon,
Impassioned dreams to shine in heart's high tide;
And make them leap in wonder bright, eftsoon
To kiss thy silver beams with loving pride.
And let fond memories of bliss come home,
Like flute's melodious wail, deep-tuned and free,
From far-off births girt with oblivious foam,
And blend with our love's silent harmony.
Moonlight and love cast their slumberous spell
Upon my soul; the sea's delightful roar,
Wave breaking on wave with a joyous lull,
After a long, thundering, splashy pell-mell,
Rouses my thoughts which e'er towards thee soar.
When Nature speaks, can human hearts be dull?

S. RANGASWAMI, M.A.

Unique

(A Sonnet with sestine doubled)

An only one ! What is that thing so rare,
Of priceless value, ne'er another like ?
No other one ! Just like Archangel Mike !
Peerless, if perfect not, yet still no pair.

Another one you say ? But not the same !
Ah no ! Unique, for pricelessness must be !
Angels many, yet diff'rent all ! So we
Just count with picture, poetry, music, name !

Better than all ! An only son ! Unique !
Priceless ! Or daughter ! E'en though many a one !
What classic words are those, " Her only son ! "
Sacrificed, taken, gone, and life left bleak—
Like many more, but still Unique ! Unique !
Whether come great, or lowly with the meek.

Greatest of all ! His only Son ! Unique !
God's Only ! Highest height of Heaven above !
Stooping to earth in mighty endless love,
The lost—despairing—one and all to seek ;
And then to depths of hell descending—Still
To preach, to rescue, those who only will !

HANNAH EMMA PALMER.

Revelation

A street, man-made, of bricks and stone,
Of buildings, many-shaped, and tall,
Huddled together—dark and sullen-grey—
Within the misty hush that follows rain.
No heights for thoughts of one who walks alone,
Are here—I fain
Would pass them swiftly, lest their gloom
Should in the lonely heart of me find room.

A street, man-made, of bricks and stone,
Of buildings, many-shaped, and tall,
Huddled together—dark, and sullen-grey ;
But this—this is not all :
For reason all unknown, I turned my head—
I was transported to a Heavenly place ;
For as I slowed my steps, and turned, behold
A patch of sky all streaked with misty gold !

Was this an error on the part of man,
A spot forgotten in the builder's plan ?
Or was it God's intention this should be,
And was this glory meant for man to see ?
This wondrous sight between two walls of stone,
Proves He is here—we walk no more alone.

G. E. PLUMRIDGE.

British Colonists

They got their lands in an honest way,
For the red man was their neighbour;
They worked them well and made them pay,
By the increment of labour.
They ate their bread with sweat on their brows
And smoked their pipes for pleasure;
For they well knew, as we since know,
That the fruits of toil are leisure.
When work was done each had some fun—
And the world has need of such men;
So I say with pride (on my father's side),
That I sprang from an Englishman.
They held their faith without offence,
And said their prayers on Sundays;
But never could see a bit of sense
In burning brush on Mondays.

They loved their God with love so true,
And with their heads so level,
That they could afford to love men, too,
In spite of the work of the devil.

They kept their word in deed and creed—
And the world has need of such men;
They were solid and strong, and have lasted long,
Real, true-born Englishmen.

W. C. POLLARD, LL.B.

Life on the Lonesome Prairies, Canada (1924)

The Pioneers lived in gentle quietness
Beside the prairie trails,
Giving themselves unselfishly,
Healing griefs and pains,
Warming, feeding, sheltering,
To those who crossed their doors,
In silence giving generously
Of their simple, frugal stores.

Not only of the body's needs
They gave a goodly share,
But many whose spirits drooped in woe
Were cheered and freed from cares.
Oh, they were friends worth having,
With their understanding hearts,
Giving many youthful dreamers
Life's elevating starts.

W. C. POLLARD, Ll.B.

Morn

Tracery of thoughts indefinable,
Tangle of dreams yet unborn,
Birds' song, and scent of the lilac,
This——is the morn.

G. E. PLUMRIDGE.

The Mystic

Not for the many, but the few, I write,
Who, like me, know of solitude's delight,
Where quiet thought may flow unhampered, till
God's hand appears directing all things to His will.

Some find this in Cathedral's columned aisle,
When trained choir awakes the solemn pile,
Where surpliced preacher oft obscures *The Word*,
Precedence giving to ritual absurd.

I do not gaze into a crystal ball,
Or try with cards or numbers dupes to thrall,
Or talk the Medium's trash, or trace the lines
On palms of idiots gulled by faker's wiles.

Yet in the forest dim, on snow-deckt peak,
I've felt the Presence, and I've heard Him speak ;
And busied in my garden, tending flowers,
I've known the help of Him Who rules all hours.

I seek my wisdom in the " Book of books ! "
Which ever offers Truth to him who looks ;
And know that there *is* Someone by my side,
Who understands each thought I would confide.

GEOFFREY B. POWELL.

What is Life?

A Sonnet

Shall I compare thee to a tender rose
Plucked from its dainty stem to be cast in fire?
Or to the beautiful strains of the sweetest lyre
Hushed in its softest pitch? Or to the close
Of a joyous dream ere the graceful pose
Of the Vision is seen?—the bow entire
Broken ere the arch is formed?—to a lofty spire
Crumbling as the Orisons sing to repose?

Or art thou a fleet-winged horse, chasing hot
The twin shadows, Hope and Desire, whose spell
Lureth thee onward, far in space, till not
A speck of their elusive wonder that's wrought
In mystic truth, meeteth thy gaze, and the knell
Is rung while yet the goal remains unsought?

S. RANGASWAMI, M.A.

Living Pictures

The red sun sinking in the west,
  Reflecting o'er a sea at rest,
A golden stream reveals to me—
  One flowing to Eternity.

The lovely moon, full overhead,
  Outlining clouds with silver thread,
Melting the dark night's heavy shroud,
  Enfolding earth like a mother proud!

O nature, capped in thy loveliest mood,
  What gems and vision to be wooed!
What artist's skill can half portray
  The dreams [1] that in thy bosom lay!

CYNTHIA RICHARDS.

---

[1] Dictionary : one definition for dreams—substance !

The Sportsman

What is there better under the sun,
Than to go for a walk and take with you a gun;
Thro' green crop and meadow, thro' cover to steal,
With a song in your heart, and your dog at your heel?

Over the hedges breaking your way,
Thinking what sport will result with the day—
Your gun at safe slope as you scramble through,
For 'tis wise to take caution, whatever you do.

Rover, the dog, is now hot on the scent;
See how he moves—scarce a blade's by him bent;
You follow behind, not daring to breathe—
He's standing transfixed—what visions you weave!

Ha! now he is off, and his music begins!
You miss your cock-pheasant—he turns round and
    grins;
You follow along, disheartened and glum;
You look at each other, and both remain dumb.

But rounding the cover, old Rover gets gay—
A rocketing pheasant is well on its way!
You miss the first barrel—despair at your heart,
You let go the second—the dog plays his part!

You pick up your bag with its precious display,
And thank all your stars for such end to the fray;
Then back to your friends—doubts and fears to allay—
To dine, smoke, and yarn—end a glorious day.

CYNTHIA RICHARDS.

A Helping Hand

How shall a grateful heart show forth
  Its thanks and highest praise
To God, for all His mercies shown
  In all His wondrous ways?

When trials sore beset the life,
  And cherished hopes seem vain;
When life sometimes seems all regret—
  The best we can't attain.

When, weak in heart, we fall a prey
  To sins which us disgust—
God leaves us not, to perish there
  For ever in the dust.

When life sometimes seems dark and drear,
  The future dark and dim,
God stretches out a loving Hand,
  And bids us look to Him:

He bids us look to Him in love,
  Forgiveness He doth send;
For having loved those dear to Him,
  He loves them to the end.

No more would life seem dark and drear,
  If unto God we'd look;
His promises are always sure—
  We find them in His Book:

And so, on Him we'll cast our care,
    Come what may, good or ill ;
We'll strive each day to serve Him well,
    And do His Holy Will.

His presence then shall go with us,
    And guide us all our years,
Until we reach the Land where He
    Doth wipe away all tears.

                        C. E. ROBOTHAM.

These Simple Things

Content is found in simple things,
    That I have learned by journeying far :
In sweet scents that the woodland brings,
    The violet dusk and misty star,
Lamp-lit cottage and sunset stain,
    Hills wearing wonder like a crown,
Still meadows and the song of rain,
    And snow-white petals blowing down.

Content lies deep in simple things,
    And release from dim foreshadowings ;
Beauty and rest in hours that fall
    In an inviolate silence over all ·
Ever their tranquil wonder stays
    And fills with keen delight my days.

                        VIOLA MACMILLAN ROBB.

Remembered Beauty

I have seen Spring's radiant freshness spread
On trees and fields and river-bed,
The Earth made an enchanted place
With fragrant grace

These eyes have seen much loveliness pass,
As wings and the south wind o'er long, cool grass,
And I have forgotten in Winter's cold
The Summer's gold.

I may forget all frail and perfect things,
The blossomy sod, a scarlet bird that sings,
But never pain's white beauty I have seen
In battered being.

Viola MacMillan Robb.

Good Night!

The day is waning. the sun sinks low,
And hushed is the birds' last call;
Silver stars peep thro' the dark blue sky,
While the pale moon shines softly o'er all.

Good night, my darling! May sweet dreams bless
Your slumber, so deep and calm.
All through the darkness may angels watch near you,
To guard you from fear and harm.

J. M. Roby.

The Nightingale

We walked thro' the glen, the sun sank low,
And the shadows grew deep and long,
The pale moon shone o'er the dew-sparkled earth,
While a nightingale poured forth his song.

He sang so softly, sweet notes of joy,
Yet sang with the pathos of pain,
Which seemed to tell of a sad lost love—
Did he know, Dear, we'd ne'er meet again?

J M. ROBY.

The Doctor

It isn't for fame, or to make a great name,
That he comforts and helps all who cal ;
In trouble or pain, he ne'er thinks of gain,
And his kindness and skill inspire all.

For others he lives, and to everyone gives
Of his best, and himself never spares ;
He endeavours to cheer, to calm every fear,
Though he's weary with other folks' cares.

When his time comes to rest, may God send him the best
Of His blessings, sweet peace from above,
And whisper, " Well done ! thy victory was won
By thy great and compassionate love."

J. M. ROBY.

Faith and Hope

When at last I am called to my Beautiful Home,
    From sorrow called unto my rest,
When softly my loved ones shall say, " She is dead,"
    And fold my cold hands o'er my breast :
Oh, when, with my glorified vision, at last
    That Beautiful Home I shall see,
Will anyone there, in that beautiful place,
    Be waiting, and watching for me ?

Yes ! There is my father who guided my steps
    With counsel—his darling I was ;
He loved me to sing of redemption and love—
    Then *HE* took my loved one away
To live in the Land that is fairer than day !
    And he will be waiting for me,
Yes, there, up above, in that Beautiful Home,
    Be waiting and watching for me.

And there is my mother, whose prayers and whose love
    Surrounded my life for so long ;
And now how I miss her, each day of my life,
    There's no one but Jesus can tell :
But we'll meet again in that Beautiful Home,
    For Jesus has said it shall be ;
Yes, she and my father, they both will be there,
    Be waiting and watching for me.

A. F. ROSE.

The Triumph of Faith

In the stillness of the wood
A silent voice was heard,
An echo of all happiness,
Like the song of a bird :

With a note of the eternal,
It uttered just one word—
" Love "—for all the World
Loves when it is stirred.

There is love in each of us
Of a pure and noble kind,
But very often it is lost
In the tangles of the mind :

So, we hurt each other sorely
When we do not hear that Word,
An echo of all happiness,
Like the song of a bird.

Love is in the trees,
Love is in the flowers,
Love is in our hearts—
Love is ours !

GEORGE RUST.

Autumn

Old age is like an autumn leaf
That changes colour
Beautifully,
Then dies,
That the earth
That gave it birth,
Again may sing,
Resurrecting from the dead
New bodies for our souls.

GEORGE RUST.

He Comes

Don't run, my soul, away, apart—
He calls! He comes! Oh, don't you hear
The throbbing of His great big Heart?
"It is I," He cries, "you need not fear."

As Peter leaped into the deep,
To Jesus walking on the water,
So leap, my soul—oh, leap! oh, leap!
Leap to Him now—oh, do not falter!

FRED W. JOHNSTON

Smiling through the Shadows

Just a little kindness,
Just some friendly deed,
Just some crumbs of comfort,
For a soul in need.
Someone over-burdened
With an unjust load,
Sick and sad and weary,
On life's stony road.

Smiling through the shadows,
Brushing tears away,
Hoping, trusting all the while
For a brighter day.
Hearts, they count for nothing,
Bruised and cast away ;
Feelings spurned and humbled pride
The order of the day.

Working, watching, waiting,
Ceaseless, thankless toil ;
Hoping, yearning, praying
For the sun to smile.
Comes a straggling sunbeam,
Shading out the gloom,
Makes a thing of beauty
The life so nearly done.

Smiling through the shadows,
Brushing tears away,
Sunshine peeping o'er the hill
From another way :

Catch it while it's lasting,
Cherish it to stay;
Take what happiness you can,
If only for to-day.

MAY ROOKER.

Over the Top!

Our brave boys in the trenches stood,
Waiting the word to go;
None knew of all they suffered there,
And none will ever know.

" Over the top, and best of luck! "
Their brave commander said;
E'en as they climbed above the trench,
They met a storm of lead.

The officer and half his men
Were left upon the field,
The rest dashed on, for Britain's sons
Will never, never yield.

The day was done, the victory won,
And friends for wounded care:
The rolls were called—but, oh, how sad!
Scarce half of them were there.

The next one in command then spoke—
" We'll bury them one by one,
And mark their graves, that all may know
   Their part was bravely done."

J. A. SALMON.

Parental Veneration

When thou wert very young, a babe,
We clothed thee in thy silken robe;
We joyed; we loved, we cherished thee,
We very nearly worshipped thee.

From pain to joy exultant found
A glow brought to our daily round,
From a thing so tiny sleeping,
From a treasure in our keeping.

No joy beholding mere repose
An æon before our eyes arose,
A treasure with a life to live,
And highest powers the world to give.

From tiny babe to little child
(And now we state it rather mild),
The days flew past, the years rolled by,
And scarcely did we know just why.

A little child, of colour fair,
Cast in a busy world of care,
To grow, to train, problems to tackle
That hold mankind in gripping shackle.

A little child of courage rare,
We pray for thee a royal share
To play thy part with noble mind,
Promoting blessing of mankind.

For soon our own generation,
Of ev'ry clime and ev'ry nation,
Will pass away, and leave behind
A heritage not very kind.

But thou art still a child so young,
From thee our thought has scarce begun ;
Yet latent promise should fulfil—
We wait the telling of thy will.

EDWARD H. SALTER.

" The World "

If you but think yourself too proud,
Cheer thyself and praise too loud,
If you but think yourself too kind,
Hate thyself for hate you'll find.
If you but try to speak fair words,
Those near about will thrust their swords ;
If you but utter slanderous speech,
And share in evil and deceit,
Those round about will praise you high,
And in their minds you'll reach the sky,
If you can mould the world in truth,
Truth ever lost, the truth of thy tooth.
If you can make the world to sin
Sin everywhere will sad begin,
In midst of these, we live and die
Those lucky born are those who fly,
And those for evil, here doth lie.

S. OSWIN DE SILVA.

N

The Human Form

This Mind that thinks, but weaves a transient web ;
This Hair that clothes the head, soon it forsakes ;
These Eyes that see afar, yet seeing, sin ;
This Ear doth list to sorrow and to joy ;
This Nose, it breathes, yet quick the breath doth fly ;
This Mouth, it speaks, yet soon its voice doth cease ;
This Face, unique, that lustre pure doth show,
It crumples, too, with wrinkles on the brow ;
These Hands that work at task, then cripple tuin ;
These Legs that walk, must homewards trudge alone :
Yea, the whole Body, but a Phantom, must
All pass, its earth to earth, its dust to dust !

S. OSWIN DE SILVA.

Work

Sweet toil and labour makes me fresh ;
My heart to work will do its best.

S. OSWIN DE SILVA.

The Words of a Man

" Mate, do that as is right, and don't do that as is
    wrong."—
An arrow of light in the darkness, the words of a Man
    who was strong.

      *   *   *   *   *

A new-made scholar of Oxford drew from the town of
    towns,
From Newman's spire and the Radcliffe, away to the
    Wiltshire downs;
Waiting a train at a junction (O that warm November
    eve !),
On a charmed hillside to wander, of the cheerless lamps
    took leave.
(From Nazareth what good cometh ? From Swindon,
    ah, Swindon, what ?
Was anywhere else his England so spoiled by a soulless
    spot ?)
Soothly his brow caressing, the spirit-breath of the night
Came with a nameless yearning, came with a deep
    delight,
Kindled anew his spirit, as the tutor called his name
From the College dais—successful . it was Love, and
    the hope of Fame.

      *   *   *   *   *

A pair on the path came walking, perhaps from the
    Railway Works,
(In workman's trousers a poet, a master of Sanskrit
    lurks !¹)

Alfred Owen Whitehouse, a native of Swindon.

And the lad, in his diamond dreaming, drew out to the
    causeway's edge,
And let a blot go by him, a noteless blot on the hedge ;
But a man in that blot, Immortal, World-passionate,
    passed along—
" Mate, do that as is right, and don't do that as is
    wrong."

        *   *   *   *   *

Boyhood to manhood ceded, Western to Eastern lands ;
On an exquisite island-jewel the scholar a teacher
    stands—
An island of forest-ruin, of forgotten monks and kings,
Where the Pilgrims Peak [1] and the pathway with
    ' Saadu,' ' Saadu,' rings.
And many a young life listened, crowd gathered, or one
    by one
On the hillside bench in the moonlight when the deeds
    of day were done,
Heirs of an ancient lineage, handsome of form and face,
Themselves in their turn to father a fairer, a finer race,
And far to the cassias golden, and the sappu's scent at
    noon,
To the palms, a silver-silent sea in the tropic moon,
To the tops of the matted mountains, to the lowlands
    leagues away,
Were the words of a workman carried from a distant
    Swindon day.
And a word in the darkness uttered shall compass the
    world in song——
" Mate, do that as is right, and don't do that as is
    wrong."

                        W. S. SENIOR.

[1] Adam's Peak, Ceylon.

Thoughts

It turns to darkness all within,
And blurs the vision's brightness:
What can this be but birth of sin
That scoffs and scorns uprightness?
Soul! conquer this, then thou hast fought
    . . . A bad thought.

It makes the world around grow dim,
And joy gives place to sadness;
With visage dour and aspect grim,
It takes the throne of gladness:
What is it, heart, that thou hast wrought?
    . . . A mad thought.

It links more closely friendship's ties,
This silent voice of sorrow;
The windows of man's soul—his eyes,
The soul's aspect they borrow;
And from those sacred depths they brought
    . . . A sad thought.

It stems all evil that may rise
Within man's inmost being;
As gleams the sun through clouded skies,
So are the soul's eyes seeing:
And what is this that thou hast sought?
    . . . A glad thought.

                   CLARRY SIMPSON.

The Meeting

Oh, little feet that pattered in the hall-way,
Oh, little hands that clutched at Mother's dress ;
Oh, baby lips, as fragrant as a rose-bud,
   That brushed my cheek so oft in sweet caress.

Ah ! could it be that I was oft so weary
   With household tasks, I had no time for play ;
I'd disappoint your baby heart, my dearie,
   By being sad when you were glad and gay ?

I still can feel the magic of your fingers,
   I still can see the love-light in your eyes ;
The memory of your roguish laughter lingers,
   As when you ran to me in glad surprise.

I know that we shall meet again, my dearest,
   When all my little tasks on earth are done ;
Close to the pearly gates you'll be the nearest—
   You'll run to meet me there, my little son.

And we shall wander through the fields of Heaven,
   And pick the blossoms there, so fresh and sweet;
And we shall weave a garland for the Master,
   And, kneeling, we shall lay it at His feet.

I know that He will smile, and softly whisper,
   " I think I love the lilies best of all ;
I used to watch them from my mother's window,
   A-blowing in the wind, so slim and tall."

And as we kneel there, in the holy silence,
A velvet rustle seems to stir the air ;
And we can hear the voices of our loved ones
Ascending up to God, in whispered prayer.

ELIZABETH B. SIMPSON.

Ode to a Cloud

Oh, thou wondrous floating mass !
Over hill and river,
Like a fleecy herd, you pass,
Wandering on for ever.

Sometimes swiftly, ofttimes slow,
Sometimes scarcely seen,
Gazing on mankind below,
Majestic and supreme.

Herded by the wind, you fly
Past the Sun, thy mother ;
Then from darkening day you hie,
Into the night, its brother.

Then, when all beneath is dark,
And the night seems long.
On you ride, to hear the lark
Burst forth in joyful song.

LEN. V. SELVA.

Reverie in Solitude

Comes a sound of the Sea in the trees to-day,
The mystical lure of the Sea;
And my heart keeps its tryst
With the the Roses—dew-kissed
In the joy of that happiest day,
That day when with troth, we pledged " Yea."

Comes a sound of the Sea in the trees to-day,
A lilt of that far-rippling Sea;
And in fancy I hear
Just the voice of my " dear ";
As we clambered those cliffs—and away,
Those Heather-clad cliffs far away.

Comes a sound of the Sea in the trees to-day,
A sound of the murmuring Sea;
And my thoughts backward swing
To those sea-gulls on wing,
As they circled the distance away,
That magical distance away.

Comes a sound of the Sea in the trees to-day,
Some sound of a billowy Sea;
And I pray God to hear
In the darkness of fear,
Until " Dawn " speed all shadows away,
Each merciless shadow away.

Comes a sound of the Sea in the trees to-day,
The rhythmical surge of the Sea;
And I feel in that surge
Some intuitive urge
Of the constancy yet—of God's way,
Immutable—ever and aye.

AMY BISHOP.

The Voice of God

Out of the silence of the night, ere dawn be sped,
The " Still small Voice of God " is heard
Like a cool hand upon a fevered brow,
And all the tumult of the day is fled.

'Neath the dim arches of some cloistered wall,
Beside the stream, where winds blow sighing o'er the
    heath—
And sometimes in the street—
We hear Him call.

And when the beauty of this bounteous world grows
    dim,
All prone we lie, in our last mortal agony,
With hands outstretched, and suppliant, whispering,
    lips,
He will have answered ere we call to Him.

K. A. STACY.

The Soul

O Soul, imprisoned in our earthly clay,
Full well I know thou longest for the day
When Death will set thee free.
Thou art, for sure, a gift of beauty rare
Given to Man, his lot on earth to share,
His realm in all Eternity.

And all through Life the Heart of Man doth reign,
Doth daze and blind, and urge him on to gain
Each worldly wish and whim :
To thee, O Soul, no Heavenly thought is given,
Death, thy Redeemer, from his mind's lightly driven,
Till Age cometh slow and grim.

Then, when, O Soul, his course of Life is run,
And " Money's " all his toils and strifes have won,
What has Man done for thee ?
A place in Heaven his money cannot buy ;
No time is for regret when Death's grim form is nigh ,
His Fate is then thy Fate, for all Eternity.

                                        E. O. SCHRSTER.

Merry Andrew's Alphabet

A is for Amy of sweet seventeen,
B is for Ball where Amy was seen ;
C is for Cheerful, her face bright and winning ;
D is for Dance, and round she went spinning.
E is for Ernest, her first love so sweet ;
F is for Friendship, when first they did meet.
G is for Glove of a delicate shade,
H is for Hand for which it was made.
I is for Inches—her waist might you span ;
J is for Jingle—the chain of her fan.
K is for Kisses—ladies like not a few ;
L is for Lips of a bright rosy hue.
M is for Merry, her eyes does she make,
N is for Nose of an exquisite shape.
O is for Opal, a bright changing colour,
P is for Promise she made to her lover ;
Q is for Questions on which she did linger,
R is for Ring which he placed on her finger.
S is for Slender form, graceful and slight ;
T is for Teeth so pearly and white.
U is for Uxorious affection now known ;
V is for Virtue, bright character shown.
W is for Willing her hand she did give him ;
X is for Xmas, the sweet carols singing ;
Y is for Yule, a cold Christmas Day ;
Z is for Zany, Merry Andrew's bright way.

CARRIE GREENWELL-SMITH.

To a Young Squirrel

Thou creature small, how quick thy motions are !
Gyrations thine—how eloquently fine !
No human art, nor eyes serene by far,
Can catch thy tricks, or match thy vision's line—
Emblem of mighty genius, whose art
And flights of fancy oft bear equipoise
With observation keen, like Dian's dart,
And skilful turns of speech and fluent voice !

K. P. SUBRAHMANIYAM.

To the Cauvery

A SONNET

Great stream, whose course is equable and clear,
How like a baby on its mother's breast,
Thy gentle tide is, nigh thy source, at rest !
But how, like torrent, next, dost thou uprear
Thy foamy crest, in dashing wild career,
Roaring and sweeping, like mad bull, opprest
By foeman's dart ! How, last, thy peace possest,
A placid pool, with heaven-averted cheer !
The like bears sway with lot of man, whose force
Is such that, at life-dawn, he is all bloom
And innocence ; but, lustier grown, he roars,
And frets, and puts on airs, and wears a plume,
Till age comes on at length, and him restores
To meek estate, which wisdom doth illume.

K. P. SUBRAHMANIYAM.

Memories

Out of the past they peep at me,
  Half-forgotten moments ;
So silently they creep at me,
  With perfume of old scents,
Those sweet times of joy and sorrow
Which grew dim when dawned the morrow.

There, in the past, I played with you,
  Half-forgotten meetings ;
How happily I strayed with you,
  So sure of your greetings
Each new day, and your dreams each night,
My own beloved friend of the light !

I walk through rooms, loved long ago ;
  Half-forgotten bookshelves,
Which yielded solace long ago,
  Peep at me like shy elves ;
Long, lovely windows beckon me—
Before me lies the tranquil sea.

The tranquil sea (how calm it seems !),
  It brings me memories, too,
Of nights when storms broke through my dreams—
  Dreams conjured up by you.
Then, stars lurked behind banks of cloud,
Now they shine in beauteous crowd.

Out of the past come mem'ries dear,
  Sweet thoughts of days gone by;
Fearing the future which draws near,
  We look back, with a sigh,
Yearning for old times, old faces,
  And those half-forgotten places.

JEAN STANTON.

Spring brings Faith

When gracious comes returning Spring,
A song wells from my heart;
Not lost is one remember'ed thing—
This faith does Spring impart.

Those friends, who erst, in other years,
Walked with me 'neath the trees—
Dear Ones I've lost, with anguished tears,
Now memory, wistful, sees,

Until with me again they pace
The flowered ways along,
And everywhere the fragrant air
Re-echoes with their song.

GRACE ROBERTSON TUTTLE.

The Merry Month of May

There's music in the murmur and the ripple of the
    stream,
There are voices full of laughter where the tumbling
    waters gleam ;
The skies above are clearest blue that yesterday were
    grey ;
It is the month of May, my sweet, the merry month of
    May !

There's a rustle in the hedges where the scented violets
    peep ;
The world all warm and rosy is awakening from her
    sleep ;
There's magic in the moonbeams and gladness in the
    day ;
It is the month of May, my sweet, the merry month of
    May !

There's a fragrance in the meadows where the bright-
    hued flowers spring,
There's a cadence in the heavens where the feathered
    songsters sing.
Oh, meet me 'neath the blossoms where the sun and
    shadows play !
It is the month of May, my sweet, the merry month of
    May !

Yet a deeper song is thrilling in the fragrance of the
    May,
A richer song than birds can sing, however sweet their
    lay ;

The song of love for man and maid, that will not pass
    away,
In the merry month of May, my sweet, the merry month
    of May.

K. A. STACY.

The Joyous Island

(TONE POEM BY DEBUSSY)

Far away,
In seas unsought by any ship of steam,
Where only wanderers sail,
Blown by soft winds from off the shores of dream.
Not wise Odysseus has sailed that sea,
Nor seen the caves
Where seagulls ever haunt, mingling their cry
With roar of waves.

Beyond the beach,
The orchards rise and grasses clothe the ground,
Where long ago from battle Arthur came
To heal his grievous wound.
And there glad folk make joyous festival;
Ships on far seas
Hear in the wind the bells of Avalon,
The Isle of Apple-Trees.

D. E. CHRISTINE TOMLIN.

Heaven

Two little lips all puckered for kisses,
Two little eyes of summer-sky blue;
Two little hands with coral-pink fingers,
Two little feet from their cover peep thru'.

Laughing and cooing, your waking hours spending,
Bubbling and chuckling, with smiles in between;
Wide-eyed in wonder at newly-found glories,
Peacefully resting when Slumber-man's been.

Sweet tiny mite, your caresses I treasure,
You are the gift it pleased God to bestow;
Deep in my heart, I thank Him in full measure
For sending down Heaven to me here below.

FREDERICA THOMPSON.

A Fish

Where wind-curled spray was creaming at the edge,
Or breaking into flake-drops, green and white,
And shapes mysterious crept through lab'rinths cool,
And burst long-brooding bubbles in their flight,
With freckled fins he dipped in rippling pools,
Or lay at rest on silver-sifted sand,
Where river buds lay clustered, fresh and cool,
And falling sunlight dripped upon the strand.

M. TOMLINSON.

Possessions

A budding flower ! As yet demurely tinted,
  Small oval face a future beauty hinted ;
Sweet dewy eyes long-lashed, and dimpled chin.
A Tuesday's child, in all things to her birthright true,
  Slight head erect and willowy frame ; one might
     construe
Of gentle grace a-plenty, too, within !
Added to this the gift of much vivacity,
Mirth, joy and mischief coupled with audacity.

A darkling pool—whose depths, as yet unprobed,
  Give glimpses, by the glancing beams enrobed,
Of something deeper, wider, haply great and simply
     wise ;
The seeds perchance of a fine nobleness of soul,
  Anon, mayhap, within the rankings of the famed to
     enrol !
And once again words from the well-known lines arise,
Here dwells the child, the father of a gentle man !

Thrice blessed am I !—Comes elfin child of happiness,
  Dancing down childhood's glades to pipes of Pan ;
Winning his way right merrily with smiles,
  Child of a thousand wiles !
Loving and wayward—and withal imperious
True child of Leo !—sometimes sweetly serious,
  Wee caraban !

Firstly and last, possessed and yet possessor—
  Owned by each one, yet owning every treasure—
Favoured of gods and kindly without measure—
  Enter the man !

VICTORIA TAYLER.

A Woodland Idyll

Blossoms, fragrance, twilight, stars, and murmuring
    melody!
Here, no sound of harshness mars the soul's tranquillity.
Here, no thought of other days, gone by, or still to come,
Can pierce the sweetly golden haze, which wraps yon
    sinking sun.
Beyond the glade a church-bell chimes—Oh, sweet and
    welcome sound!—
The woodlands laugh, the brooklets sing, and Heaven is
    all around.

What is the song the river sings, in harmony so rare?
I hear a sound of blue-bird's wings, or sighs of maiden
    fair.
How came those purple violets, like a slumb'ring dream,
    to lie
Just sheltered by the beech-trees' shade from reckless
    passers-by?
What are those whispers in the glade? Whose was the
    voice which spoke?
Ah! true, yon dancing woodland maid is child of fairy
    folk.

Oh! stay then, in this peaceful spot, where mirth and
    song are sweet,
And I, on bed of moss and fern, will lie here at your feet.
Forget the years which brought those many lines of
    care and pain,
For we two, in one glorious hour, can live them o'er
    again.

I'll sing you songs of woodland vales, beneath bright
 summer skies,
And you shall tell the wondrous tale I see within your
 eyes.

Sunshine, music, moonlight, dreams, and blissful sweet
 content !
Ah ! God is good, and you, it seems, to me from Heaven
 were sent.
We'll stay till od'rous wood-flowers, on their mosses,
 sleeping lie,
Till, thro' the parted leaves, we see the diamond-studded
 sky ;
Till glow-worms light their lanterns, and the smile of
 day depart,
Till the first sweet, silver dew-drops fall in the purple
 violet's heart.

DOROTHY TENNANT.

Seasons of the Soul

The Seasons four pass o'er the Soul,
Their ways and powers 'fore her unroll;
Their deaths and their lives, in peace and in strife,
Are sent by the Maker of Wisdom, with Life.

The Spring comes bounding, full of hope,
All fresh with youth's undaunted dreams:
Where showers of April wash the slope
Up spring the shooting stem, I ween.

The snowdrop and the violet, both,
With tender power break forth from earth,
In coloured glory, voiceless troth,
Devoted to man's need and worth.

The birds of dawning glory sing
The song of Heavenly joy below,
And rise above, on piercing wing,
To call for answer, high and low.

So in my soul, the Spring of Life,
From out of Chaos, deep and dark,
Hath risen in love, found peace in strife,
And known the Pilot of the barque.

Within my Soul, a Voice did speak,
Within my heart a tear-drop start,
That from the ground a seed, so weak,
Sprang up and grew to live its part.

W. Timms.

Disturbed Tranquillity

'Twas eventide when through the dell
I wandered, late in Spring,
And heard the airy music tell
Of Nature—precious thing !
I wandered long, until, at length,
I reached a little gate,
And there I spied, in puny strength,
A memory of hate.

I plucked the little emblem red,
And thought of years gone by,
When Mankind, torn by hate to shreds,
Discarded truth—to die !
It spoke to me—yet uttered not
One word—but bent its head,
As memories of rifle-shot
Again filled one with dread.

Once more I saw the wooden cross
So primitive and bare ;
And, midst the conflicts' gory dross,
We stood—in silent prayer.
A sign of peace !—that shallow grave,
To one escaped from hell,
A shattered, broken body ; save—
The soul that served so well.

The world toiled on in darkness then,
Its course lost for an age,
When jealousy rich reason penned,
And locked with empty rage.

How long I stood I cannot think,
But—when I looked again,
The poppy had begun to shrink,
Ashamed—like me—of then.

LESLIE TUCKER.

Moths

Into the lamp of life,
Bewildered moths, we fly,
And know not why.

Gaily we flutter in its flame,
Upborne by rainbow dreams,
Till vain our vision seems.

Then, bruised, burned, broken,
We fall to die,
In dust, forgotten lie.

GRACE ROBERTSON TUTTLE.

Empire Honour

Unfurl our glorious banner
  Of freedom, truth and light,
And let it fly both wide and high
  For courage in the right.

Our fathers fought for freedom,
  We reap what they have sown ;
But oh, there's need for nobler deed
  Than yet our race has known.

For sin has still its strongholds
  That drag our Empire down ;
They dog her track, and hold her back
  From heritage and crown,

Arise ! ye sons of Empire,
  In all your pride of youth,
And work and fight with all your might
  For *purity* and *truth*.

Then God and King and Empire
  Shall own and bless the day,
When, free from wrong, we shall be *strong*
  To tread the upward way.

JESSIE L. THOMAS.

Faith Unalloyed

D'you remember the days of our childhood, when we
and our young confrères
Thought the royal'st road to Victory was to be good,
and to say our prayers?
At work, at school, or at playtime, this belief we would
fondly hail;
Success would crown our efforts and hopes—we should
not *always* fail.

Comes Life with its disillusions, its bitterness and its
sighs,
Its cruel, if dignified, Silence that ne'er answers our
endless WHY'S:
Love seems to lose its meaning, Honour turns round and
laughs,
Truth becomes a mockery, and Beauty simply chaffs.

If you've still a grain of your childhood's Faith, be sure
you hold to it tight!
Never mind if others may jibe at it, so long as it serves
YOU right.
From Beauty and Love it'll wipe the spots, Bitterness
it will lame,
Honour and Truth will still look good—will help you
to play the game.

And armed with man's most sacred possession, through
Darkness and Sorrow and Sin,
You will ride a Daring Crusader—whether you lose or
win.

"VINEGARR."

The Enchanted Woods

In little remote spots by a stream,
Lovely Primroses and Violets dream ;
They dream of things so rare,
Of castles built in the air,
And of the Sun and its golden beams.

Beneath the golden Sun's pouring rays,
Great large Oaks and Fir-trees tall, calmly sway
They softly sway in the breeze,
Reaping a song of the trees,
A happy song of by-gone days.

The sighing winds repeat the gay song
That taught the Birds the right from the wrong
The stream, as if enchanted, ,
Bubbles and rushes on,
Onward to the setting Sun, so red.

On banks, each side, Forget-me-nots thrive ;
But the King-Cups have not yet arrived.
The Cuckoo is returning,
The Owl is complaining,
For night covers the Wood with a sigh.

All silence reigns in this enchanted Wood,
Where all Birds, Flowers and Trees are good
They rest in peace with God.
Where man has never trod,
In the beauty of this Enchanted Wood.

T. M. VAUGHAN.

This is Remembering

Across the lands and leagues of sea between,
    By far, imagined ways, familiar grown,
    Ten thousand times my searching heart has flown,
The while my lips engaged with prayer have been,
Unto that grave which I have never seen,
    Where lies, in foreign soil, unnamed, unknown,
    A sentient dust within th' insensate sown—
Where—where, in all those fields again so green?

With splendid words they seek to comfort me:
    That God, Who rules, regards His fixed stars
    No more than one lost grave, or one heart's scars
I do not know. I only know that he,
    My son, long years ago was small and sweet....
    To kiss, as then, the covers at his feet!

                                MARGARET WADE.

God's Love

Time and tide wait for no man,
But the love of the Father can
Find you in the uttermost depths,
And out of the abyss bring you to rest,
To where flowers bloom—
Into His home, at the sunset hour,
Into His heart, by occult power.
He will fold his arms around you,
Hold you tight, you will never rue.
You will walk in power where you trod in fear;
Fear you, the beauty of the Spring will bring
Healing and love on an angel's wing;
You will behold the dawn of day
Clear from the mountains the mist away;
Out of the blue will come forth a song,
Rising and falling, in cadence long.
So for you will come the morning hour,
When the Father's love will enfold you, Dear:
You will ascend, with a son's right,
The stairs that lead to the Father's sight.

M. P. Watson.

Death or Sleep

Be of good cheer! the way unfolds,
The dew drops gently on the rose:
The heart of man is ever faint
Before the day has reached its close.
Still onward goes the setting sun,
The west is radiant in its glow;
On earth the weary eyelids close,
Man, wrapped in slumber, doth repose.
The spirit, free, it onward goes:
Angels await it here, it bring
In safety to the Father's wing.

M. P. WATSON.

Good Thoughts

Good thoughts are rare pearls, rich and manifold,
  Embedded in the ocean of the mind:
A concentrated force, and, though untold,
  Disseminating, free, and unconfined.

They radiate their beauty near and far,
  They smooth the jagged edge of primal things;
Their potency is broadcast, and they are
  For ever borne on never-flagging wings.

Born of the Spirit, spirit-like they flee,
  Where minds can intercept the good they teach :
Their destination is infinity,
  And ever out, and ever up they reach.

Some from the ocean's depth have been redeemed,
  Have passed from age to age, and still have known
The sweetness of their truth admired, esteemed,
  Revered, remembered whither they have gone.

Vibrating through the eye, or through the ear,
  Soon would they find the understanding heart,
Their beauty growing physically clear,
  Though psychically moulded from the start.

Thus two worlds blend, and thus they interact—
  Where men have time to think the spirit glows ;
Like must inevitably like attract, ,
  And so the sum of Earthly goodness grows.

But whether men will think, that they may write—
  Or whether ponder, that they should converse—
Or only deeply meditate, and quite
  In their sublimer thought ego disperse—

It is quite certain that the spark divine,
  Disseminates a holier light abroad ;
And every thought will scintillate and shine,
  Where spirit seeks its own, and Man his God.
                                DOUGLAS WEMYSS.

Posthumous

He lay upon the battlefield,
  His forehead tinged with red;
A smile was on his childish face
  Although the spark had fled.

He clutched a picture in his hand
  (Remnant of long ago);
No one may tell the wealth contained
  In hearts which pure love know!

A faded picture, lock of hair,
  Can ease a passing mind;
So we in peace can travel on,
  And leave a world behind.

The terrors were frustrated when
  He passed the final mile,
For, with these memories to cheer,
  He faced them with a smile.

Oh, would that I could paint a scene
  Or write an epic rare!
But pen nor paint could not complete
  The story written there.

A sacrifice of life and love
  To save a cause unknown;
Yet selfishness and prejudice,
  We cherish and condone:

They buried him upon the field ;
But he will never know it—
Although a line he never penned,
" At heart he was a poet."
HENRY B. WILKINSON (B.S.M., A.E.F.)

Autumn Leaves

" I'm growing tired of my green dress," said the proud
    old Maple-tree ;
" I think I'll ask the Fairies what they can do for me."
Her message to the Fairies was carried by the breeze,
And soon the little Fairy folk were there to paint the
    leaves.
But when they all were painted, in colours bright and
    gay,
The naughty wind came creeping up, and blew them
    all away.
FLORENCE L. WILSON.

In the Garden

I walked through the garden at early dawn ;
My heart was sad and my thoughts forlorn ;
As I trudged along with low-bowed head,
My very soul within seemed dead.
" Good morning, dear friend ! I beg you, Pray,
Tell why you're feeling so sad to-day."
A dear little face looked up into mine—
A pansy that shone like the Christ-child, Divine.
" Come, tell me your secret," another voice said ;
" A daisy won't tell—please trust me," she pled.
" Pee-eeved ! Pee-eeved " seemed to come to my ear,
As though I were taunted by some friend dear :
A little grey bird flew down from a tree,
For a moment I felt as ashamed as could be.
" Cheer-up ! Cheer-up ! " was the next that I heard—
I lifted my head to smile at a bird.
It seemed that all nature was calling to me,
From the wee little flower to the bird in the tree.
" Forgive me, dear Father," I prayed to the skies
" Thy creatures have shown where to find Paradise."

FLORENCE L. WILSON.

The Task of To-day

There's a job which has to be tackled and done,
   Requiring much patience—p'r'aps skill ;
It's been waiting for months, but still is undone,
   Because of " To-morrow, I will."

" To-morrow," the world glibly says, " never comes,"
   So why put the job off to-day ?
Time, like the tide ebbing, away from us runs,
   Chance seldom again comes our way.

Should only *one* soul gather comfort and cheer
   If the job be done now, and done well,
Then it's worth doing to-day, though it may cost us
     dear,
   For the value we never can tell.

" To-morrow, I will "—and the soul may be gone
   To the realms where the words, " Well done ! "
Are praise given those who, though all tired and worn,
   Mastered tasks which many oft shun.

So up, man, and get at the task—now—to-day.
   Forgetting yourself in the work !
To-day is for him who gives sunshine away,
   To-morrow, the day of a ' shirk.'

THEO WILTSHIRE.

Give Me the Open Country

Give me the open country,
  Give me a place in the sun ;
Give me a song, to help me along,
  And show me the work to be done.

Give me a pal to love me ;
  Someone who'll understand ;
Who'll always be near, to comfort and cheer,
  And give me a helping hand.

Save me a cosy corner
  For when my life is spent ;
Through all the while, give me a smile,
  And I shall be content.

                    EDWARD A. WOOLVER.

The Garden of Roses

I dreamed that I walked in a garden of roses ;
　Lovely they were, and all covered with dew ;
But the beauty and colour, the scent of the roses,
　All faded away when you came into view.

The rays of the sun caught the gold of your tresses,
　Making a halo around your dear head ;
The blush on your cheeks from the wind's soft caresses,
　Brought back all the colour the roses had shed.

I, and the birds, and the flowers, all paid homage,
　And for our reward had a glimpse of your smile ;
Now my poor heart will be ever in bondage—
　The love that you wakened will live all the while.

Surely the gods had decreed I should meet you,
　Fairest and sweetest that ever I've seen ?
But when, in my madness, I went forth to greet you,
　You faded away—and I woke from my dream.

I'll always remember that garden of roses,
　And always have dreams that never can be ;
But I want you to know, in my heart there reposes
　A picture of you, and a sweet memory.

　　　　　　　　　EDWARD A. WOOLVER.

The Seasons' Message

Lo! Spring is here!
The time of singing birds, blue skies and wakening
    flowers;
    The music of the weir,
And rushing of wind through the trees as the buds
    unfold.
    So, too we hear
The echo of a gentle voice, saying, " Rejoice!
    He is not here:
Christ is risen." Easter lilies their message tell.

    'Neath Summer skies,
The rose casts forth its fragrance on the gentle breeze,
    The lily vies
In scattering sweetness over the sun-kissed vales.
    'Neath Easter skies
The " Rose of Sharon " once spread *His* fragrance
    over a world
    Of sin and sighs,
Giving pardon, cheer, and comfort—a Saviour dear.

    The Autumn brings
A store of golden fruit; the ripening crops
    In the valleys sing;
And through the whispering trees, shines the harvest
    moon.
    Lord, may we bring
In the Autumn of life our fruits of the Spirit
    To Thee, and sing
As the twilight gathers, " O Lord, abide with me."

O Winter, wild,
Of howling winds and storm-tossed seas, when frozen
    earth
    With snow is piled,
What lesson can't thou teach the worn, weary ones of
    earth ?
    In Winter wild,
When our souls are tossed on the stormy sea of life,
    O " Master," mild,
    " Peace " to our troubled hearts as we breast
the wave.

                  GRACE WOODRUFFE.

The Prodigal's Mother

When the road is steepest,
And the furrow deepest,
I know whose smile
Would brighten each mile—My Mother's

If I wander far away,
From path of virtue stray,
I know whose love
Pleads to God above—My Mother's !

When, repentant, I turn
To where home-fires burn,
I know whose kiss
Would mean to me bliss—My Mother's !

                  GRACE WOODRUFFE.

Eventide

On Poet's Walk, Somerset

I wander'd alone, when shadows fell softly,
And gazed at the setting sun ;
From the old grey church in the valley
Bells chimed for evensong.

I sat musing awhile, in the twilight,
Of the poets, in bygone days,
Walking this way in the fading light,
While the ebb-tide flow'd in the bays.

Their memories hallow this fine old hill,
Now bathed in crimson and gold ;
Waves break over the grey stones still,
As in days long past, and told.

The church bells had now ceased chiming
Their call to evening prayer ;
I entered the dim, old building,
And joined in the worship there.

" Father, hear us, we pray Thee ;
In Thy mercy keep us this night
Safe from all danger, and grant us
At eventide, peace and light."

GRACE WOODRUFFE.

Jutland

[*Lovingly dedicated to Harry Yeo, who was killed
in the Battle of Jutland.*]

Strange thoughts, as lodgers, dwell in mankind's mind ;
As vet'ran sailors, tell true stories all,
Of stirring facts, of battles left behind,
Of fights at sea amidst the cannon's brawl.
And now they'll tell of Jutland's famous name—
Tell of the fight there fought on churned sea-foam ;
Of guns on ships, all belching ruddy flame,
On alien water-ways afar from home ,

Of battle-cruisers launched from distant shore—
Huge floating batteries made of toughen'd steel ;
Of bursting shells that hit, with hellish roar,
Great ships, and shattered them from stem to heel ;
Of ships of war that swiftly sank below—
No matter that each Fleet was called *The Grand* !—
With officers and men, both friend and foe,
Who fought against, or for Great Britain's Land ;

Of others that, sore crippled in the fray,
Half-sinking, limped outside the battle's rim ;
Of those, again, though having fought all day,
That watched the night through, till the sun's first glim,
All ready once again stern fight to show,
With guns that longed once more to wake in strife,
And stubborn crews—all ratings, high and low—
Prepared for Britain's sake to yield their life.

Of such things they will tell, and many more
Concerning that stern fight on Jutland's wave:
But though all's told, there's naught that can restore
Those who died there, the gallant and the brave.

THOMAS WOODS.

A Vacation Poem

Through autumn woods where trees are brown,
Amongst the hills above the town,
The castle and its mystery stand,
For men to probe throughout the land.

The pathways to that ancient place
Are thick with weeds and ivy lace;
And every corner seems to share
The ghostly echoes living there.

The moss collects where roses grew
In varied plots to paint the view;
And mist for ever moves around
The ramparts of the haunted ground.

Across the tragic castle walls
The shadows dance when evening falls,
And phantoms on the terrace play
Amongst the debris and decay.

Up broken stairs the breezes ride
Through webs that cling on every side,
And down each passage weird and long
The night-bird sends his mournful song.

Beside the porch a quaking ghost
In silence keeps his solemn post
And dreamy bats that venture late
Molest his realm and scorn his fate.

The banquet hall for splendid feast,
Can charm no more with tasty beast;
And in each long-forgotten room
No light contrives to match the gloom.

Through broken roof and wretched door
The storms of every season pour;
And year by year the spiders creep
Across the glory fell asleep.

HENRY WHITWORTH.

Sad Farewells

I never cast a flower away,
The gift of one who cared for me,
A little flower—a faded flower—
But it was done reluctantly.

I never looked a last adieu
To things familiar, but my heart
Shrank, with a feeling almost pain,
E'en from their lifelessness to part.

I never spoke the word, "farewell,"
But with an utterance faint and broken,
And heart-sick yearning for the time
When it should never more be spoken.

PETER K. WALKER.

Sailing

Have you ever been a-sailing on the merry, dancing sea,
Wi' th' wind upon your weather-beam and water o'er
    your lee ?
Have you ever felt the salt sea-spray fly smacking in
    your face
When you're heeling gunwales under and you're leading
    in a race ?

Have you ever been a-sailing in half a howling gale
When seas are running mountains high, an' there's water
    on your sail ?
Have you ever heard the water hiss beneath your knife-
    like keel,
Watched the sea-gulls just behind you as they circle,
    glide and wheel ?

Have you ever been a-sailing on the golden sea of
    dreams.
When Lady Moon, with shining face, pours down her
    silvery beams ?
Will you ever sail your storm-tossed soul into that Port
    of Rest
Which lies out to the westward, midst the Islands of
    the Blest ?

                              PETER K. WALKER.

" Agen "

In my ' young youth ' I always thought
(In fact, I was distinctly taught)
That that small word, ' again,'
Should always rhyme with 'rain.'

Now, after all these years, I find
I've blundered up some alley blind :
The word ' again ' should coupled be
With some such word as ' men,' you see.

But who has dared this awful thing
To say, to shout, and even sing ?
Come closer, boys and list to me--
'Twas none other than the B. B. C. !

So now let's look around and see
What this may mean to you and me
One instance comes at once to mind.
Which could apply to all mankind

The words are, " Mother's grief and pain ". . .
" Oh, welcome, dearest Father, welcome back again "
But now it must be " grief and pen,"
To make it match that word, ' agen.'

" Agen " we have in that sweet hymn,
" A few more years shall roll ".
Line four, last verse, we now must pen,
" That we with Him may ren " !

A number of these instances
Could come into my ditty,
But just these two are quite enough
To prove it is a pity

The B. B. C. do not recall
That age-old tag which listeners all
Call up, forget, and then bemoan :
That tag is this, " Leave well alone."

H. O. WARD

Royal Chelsea Pensioners

(Republished and Abridged)

Beloved is that hallow'd ground, that sacred Home at
  Chelsea found !
There in the past men sat to smoke
Men who had fought mid battle's glow in Land of
  Maple-Leaf, I trow,
And shared Wolfe's master-stroke
From fields of Spain alight with flame, from Waterloo
  and Alma, same,
They reached that Home, to stay ;
From farther lands, too, o'er the sea, they came from
  fields where, all agree,
They won the fearsome fray.
In Zulu War some had a share, with Colley stood at
  Juba, there,
To face what might befall !
Here shelter'd Wood's staunch men, and then came
  Wolseley's, Roberts', Haig's brave men,
True heroes one and all !
In every climate 'neath the sun they fought since
  Blenheim's fight was won,
On plain or mountain crest ;
And one and all can story tell, how, far from home,
  across the swell,
They left their dead to rest

Thomas Woods.

Sursum Corda

Oh, have you risen in dawn's grey hours,
And wandered to some faery place,
And pressed your flushed and burning face
Among the dew-besprinkled flowers?
And have you ever heard the song
That rises to the listening sky—
A wordless melody, a sigh—
That soothes away the grief which long
Has held your heart and mind?
And did you feel that all the air
Was filled with hands that took your care
And flung it .wide upon the wind?
Oh, surely you have heard the strain,
And lifted up your head to hear
How through the pine-stems thin and clear
It steals, and drives away your pain?
And at the faery music's call
You spring up, and forget your care,
And see once more the flowers fair,
The gleaming, rushing water-fall,
And all the thousand lovely things
That you were blind to for so long.—
Thank God, for He has made you strong,
And raised your soul on beauty's wings.

ELIZABETH M. YOUNG.

CPSIA information can be obtained at www.ICGtesting.com
Printed in the USA
BVOW10s1210290715

410957BV00017B/164/P